The
Antiques Magpie

Also available from Icon Books
The Science Magpie
The Nature Magpie

The
Antiques Magpie

**A fascinating compendium of absorbing
history, stories, facts and anecdotes
from the world of antiques**

MARC ALLUM

Published in the UK in 2013 by
Icon Books Ltd, Omnibus Business Centre,
39–41 North Road, London N7 9DP
email: info@iconbooks.net
www.iconbooks.net

Sold in the UK, Europe and Asia
by Faber & Faber Ltd, Bloomsbury House,
74–77 Great Russell Street,
London WC1B 3DA or their agents

Distributed in the UK, Europe and Asia
by TBS Ltd, TBS Distribution Centre, Colchester Road,
Frating Green, Colchester CO7 7DW

Distributed in Australia and New Zealand
by Allen & Unwin Pty Ltd,
PO Box 8500, 83 Alexander Street,
Crows Nest, NSW 2065

Distributed in South Africa by Book Promotions,
Office B4, The District, 41 Sir Lowry Road,
Woodstock 7925

Distributed in Canada by Penguin Books Canada,
90 Eglinton Avenue East, Suite 700,
Toronto, Ontario M4P 2YE

ISBN: 978-184831-603-4

Typeset in Adobe Caslon by Marie Doherty

Printed and bound in the UK
by CPI Group (UK) Ltd, Croydon CR0 4YY

For Lisa and Tallulah

Only the curious find life a mystery
—Anon

ABOUT THE AUTHOR

Marc Allum is a freelance art and antiques writer, broadcaster, consultant and lecturer based in Wiltshire. He has been a miscellaneous specialist on the *Antiques Roadshow* since 1998 and has appeared on several other television and radio programmes. Marc spent sixteen years as a London-based auctioneer and has written and contributed to numerous books. He writes regularly for magazines and has a passion for playing the bass guitar and tinkering with large engines.

CONTENTS

INTRODUCTION

antique, *n.*
a collectable object such as a piece of furniture or
work of art that has a high value because of its age and
quality …

magpie, *n.* and *adj.*
B. *adj. (attrib.)*
1. Magpie-like: with allusion to the bird's traditional
reputation for acquisitiveness, curiosity, etc.; indiscrimi-
nate, eclectic, varied.

—*Oxford English Dictionary*

[Author's note: In my opinion 'high value' is not a
definitive reason for an object being of antique status.]

We are by nature acquisitive. We all collect. It's not something that is always physically manifested in the sense of a
stamp album or a collection of Pre-Raphaelite paintings.
You can collect just about anything, even quite intangible
things like thoughts. I can't remember jokes but I have a
friend who is a walking anthology. It's all in his head; he's
a collector of humour.

Collecting is complicated, an infusion of many vari-
ables drawn from our fragility, insecurity and desire, driven
by the need to leave a mark on the world, validate, educate
and elucidate. For some, it simply complicates matters;
we are, after all, just temporary custodians with a limited period of time with which to play out our acquisitive

tendencies, unlike the great museums and institutions, which offer a comforting permanence.

I'll try to keep it as real as possible but within these pages you'll have to deal with various notions that might at first seem surprising. You thought that you were buying a book about antiques, and you are, but it's all much more complicated than it first appears, mainly because what is tangible in the world of art and antiques is often just a physical manifestation of something far more ephemeral and more likely based on historical interpretations of religion, death, science and fashion. That's why you'll find some rather esoteric headings such as 'Mythical Objects' and 'The First Museums'. These will hopefully help to put our (and by 'our' I'm referring to the human race as a whole) acquisitive habits and idiosyncratic accumulative tendencies into perspective.

We need history, it gives us a sense of worth, solid points of reference along which to place the milestones of time, a ledger of the lessons we continually fail to learn. These milestones are the buildings, the bones, the photographs, the middens, the flint arrowheads and the golf ball on the moon. We need memories, and these objects form the bridges in time that reinforce our 'souvenirs'.

I started collecting as a youngster, probably around the age of nine. There was an innocence to the pursuit at that tender age, one that I miss. As you get older you acquire more and more emotional baggage, more life experience and it forces you to readdress the way you look at life and artefacts. This can be a trap for the serious collector, as mortality and objects are closely associated. As a boy, I would leave home on my bicycle, a spade strapped to the crossbar, cycle several miles and spend hours digging an old bottle dump. The dark, cinder-blackened earth that characterised 19th-century dumps belied the potential treasures that I eagerly sought: the Cods and Hamiltons (types of bottles) that I loaded into my father's old canvas rucksack ready for the long slog home. I washed them in a plastic bowl in the garden, scoured off the rust stains and arranged them on shelves in my bedroom.

Now, it's different. As I grew older, the objects began to acquire voices; they started to speak to me. The bottles were no longer inanimate objects fashioned from silica, sodium carbonate and lime. My desire to acquire objects with louder voices grew, and instead of mineral water and sauce bottles I wanted 18th-century claret bottles resplendent with seals. Now I wanted to know *who* had owned them. And there you have it; I had caught the disease that is antiques. There is no known cure.

Marc Allum, 2013

All art is useless.
—Oscar Wilde, *The Picture of Dorian Gray*

MYTHICAL OBJECTS

*Objects are what matter. Only they carry
the evidence that throughout the centuries something
really happened among human beings*
—Claude Levi Strauss

It's easy for us. With centuries of research and archaeology behind us, and with the marvellous resources of museums and institutions now at our disposal, we are to a great extent able to find out what most things are, or we at least have the foresight to save things for future generations to re-examine. We live for history and, consequently, history lives for us. That's not to say that we aren't constantly discovering new things about history and objects; it's just that we have a great accumulated knowledge at our disposal.

Imagine when things were different and a person going about their everyday life – a 15th-century serf for example – had absolutely no idea what a fossil was. When your daily existence revolves around a few important precepts such as God, eating to stay alive and paying your tithes, it's not difficult to see how your Christian view of the world might have been steadfastly instilled in your head to discount any notion of an alternative other than the sure-fire stone depictions of Purgatory and Hell carved around your local church door. So, what did the serf think a fossil was? It's an idea that grew in my head many years ago, taking objects from prehistory and antiquity and trying to find out what people thought they were, as opposed to what we now know them to be.

As a consequence of this fascination, the 'Enlightenment' room in the British Museum is one of my favourite spaces in the entire world. Admittance should be strictly limited to people wearing 18th-century dress. Gazing at the wondrous objects in the cases is as close as it's possible to come to the individuals who formed our understanding of the world and the objects in it. Here you can gaze upon Dr John Dee's (1527–1608/9) obsidian mirror, an Aztec artefact used by the famous occultist and 'consultant' to Elizabeth I to summon spirits. Dee, like many intellectuals, tried to reconcile the divide between science and magic; these are some of the most enigmatic display cases in museum history and you too can absorb the energy of these powerful artefacts. The once-mythical status of these objects imbues them with a special meaning for collectors. Here are a few of my mythical favourites:

Unicorn's horn

The unicorn, a legendary supernatural creature usually depicted in European mythology as a white horse with a long spiral horn emanating from its forehead, was the most important and idealised mythical creature of the Middle Ages. It could only be captured by a virgin and the horn, said to be made of a material called alicorn, was thought to have magical properties including the treatment of diseases and as an antidote to poison. As a result, 'unicorns' horns' that appeared on the market had great value, and were fashioned into amulets, cups and medicinal preparations. However, we now know that these 'horns' were actually narwhal tusks. The narwhal is a species of whale that lives in Arctic waters. The tusk is in fact a tooth and in some rare cases a narwhal will grow two such teeth.

The 'horns' were of such high value that they were traded by Vikings and coveted by royalty, often taking the form of chalices that were used to divine poisoned drinks. The Imperial Treasury in Vienna has on display the imperial crown, orb and sceptre of Austria, the latter fashioned from a unicorn's, or rather narwhal's, horn. Objects fashioned from narwhal tusks were favourites among blue-blooded collectors and power-hungry despots – they were the most likely to be poisoned – and were the type of object essential to any cabinet of curiosities.

The myth of the unicorn continued to be believed well into the 18th century, although scholars had largely debunked the magical origins of the horns by the mid-17th century.

One famous representation of a unicorn was constructed by the mayor of Magdeburg, Germany, Otto von Guericke, in 1663. Like many towns needing an attraction, he bolstered tourism by constructing what he claimed to be a unicorn, from the fossilised bones of a prehistoric rhinoceros and mammoth found in a local cave. It's still there to this day.

Much valued among collectors, an antique 'unicorn's horn' can realise thousands but beware, narwhals are an endangered species and the trading of their mythical teeth is now governed by the CITES convention.

Hag stone
This is one for the low-budget collector and one of the first mythical objects I acquired; in fact, you can pick them

up for free. A hag stone, also known as a witch stone, druid stone or sometimes adder stone, is basically a stone with a naturally occurring hole through it. They were and still are regarded by many as powerful amulets, although the idea that they are formed from the hardened saliva of serpents has been discredited. Hag stones have lots of applications. They are portals to the faery realm and provide a window to another dimension. Look through one and you can see faeries and witches. Nail one to your stable door and it will protect your horses from being 'hag-ridden' (ridden by witches and returned in a poor state of health) at night. Milk your cow through one and the milk will not curdle. Hag stones are an antidote to poison and a cure for various ills. Thread one on a string and hang it around your child's neck and they won't have nightmares. Quite useful all in all – and free to any ardent beachcomber.

Tektites

Controversy still surrounds the origins of tektites but it generally seems to be accepted that they are the product of meteorite impacts on the earth's surface, which, millions of years ago, forced a mixture of earthly material and meteoric debris back into space. This debris then re-entered the atmosphere in the form of glasseous stones ranging from a few grams to several kilos. Not dissimilar to their terrestrial counterpart obsidian, but somewhat unnatural in appearance with a variety of shapes and colours ranging from black to translucent green, our ancestors obviously realised that these strange-looking pebbles were unearthly and attributed them with magical properties. They have been found in archaeological contexts dating back tens of thousands of years, worked as tools and utilised as jewellery.

They generally occur in four main 'strewn fields': the North American strewn field, associated with the Chesapeake Bay impact crater; the Ivory Coast strewn field, associated with the Lake Bosumtwi crater; the Central European strewn field, associated with the Nördlinger Ries crater; and the Australasian strewn field, with no known associated crater. An anomaly is Libyan Desert Glass (LDG), similarly found over a wide area in the Libyan desert, ranging from green to yellow in colour. It's thought that this may have been formed by an aerial explosion, but the jury still seems to be out on this one. Recently, it was discovered that the scarab in Tutankhamun's pectoral was in fact made of Libyan Desert Glass, perhaps suggesting that the Egyptians valued its otherworldliness. Other historical associations include Chinese references dating from the 10th century where the writer Liu Sun refers to them as *Lei-gong-mo* or 'Inkstone of the Thundergod'.

Small tektite examples are relatively inexpensive and can be purchased on the internet; to hold one is an experience that cannot be judged in monetary terms – but beware fakes.

Elf-shot
We have plenty of evidence of our ancient ancestors, often in the form of stone tools. However, the existence of such artefacts was unfathomable to our not-so-distant relatives and they often attributed their presence to strange events or supernatural beings. Many maladies and complaints,

such as rheumatism and arthritis, were historically blamed on beings from the faery realm firing arrows known as elf-shot. (They were demons rather than fairy-tale characters.) These apparently caused all sorts of maladies in both humans and animals. The obvious proof for this was the Neolithic and Mesolithic flint arrowheads left by the 'elves'. These were then used as protective amulets; some were mounted in silver and worn around the neck. Alternatively, an arrowhead might be placed in water, whereupon it would supposedly produce a philtre or curative drink. Mounted examples from antiquity are rare and much sought after by collectors.

Similarly, ancient stone axe heads, slingshot stones and fossils such as belemnites were thought to be thunderbolt cores. They were also used as protective amulets and have frequently been found in tombs and graves and built into the walls of medieval buildings.

Bezoar stone

Derived from the Persian *pād-zahr*, meaning 'antidote', a bezoar stone, like many of its mythical counterparts, was thought to be an antidote to poison. The 'stones' are formed in the stomach or intestines of most living creatures (the most sought-after come from a type of Persian goat) and are composed of indigestible matter such as hair and plant fibre. Bezoars can take on a crystalline form and although we know that they are ineffective in dealing with poison generally, there may be some truth in the fact that certain varieties are capable of absorbing arsenic.

Bezoars were much-treasured objects and historical specimens from the royal courts and *Wunderkammers* (wonder rooms) of Europe are often ornately mounted with precious metals and jewels or housed in wonderful cabinets. Antique specimens are eagerly sought; so too are their man-made equivalents, Goa stones, named after their place of origin. Usually made of a clay, crushed ruby, gold leaf, shell, musk and resin conglomerate, Goa stones were invariably contained within an ornate silver or gold filigree holder. They were immensely valuable and a 16th- or 17th-century example was worth far more than its weight in gold. Consequently, they are still very valuable today.

NB: The trading of modern bezoars from endangered species is common in the Far East. The internet is awash with fakes and illegally sourced stones – beware!

Toad stone and tongue stone

The Lepidotes was a fish that lived in the Jurassic and Cretaceous periods. Its peculiar button-shaped teeth were used for crushing molluscs and they are preserved in the fossil record as shiny button-like nodules. At some juncture in history, these fossilised teeth became associated with the toad, a much-maligned and ostracised creature commonly associated with witchcraft. The stones were thought to be present in the heads of toads and extricable by a number of different methods, including sitting the toad on a red cloth.

The stones apparently warmed up when placed in the proximity of poison (surprise, surprise) and were often mounted in gold rings or in jewellery, now prized by collectors. The stones can be easily purchased on the internet but it's the magical association that's important to serious collectors. Shakespeare's reference in *As You Like It* sums up the general feeling about toads in the 16th century:

> Sweet are the uses of adversity;
> Which, like the toad, ugly and venomous,
> Wears yet a precious jewel in his head.

Sharks' teeth, which are among the most commonly occurring fossils on the planet, have a similar meaning in historical terms: they were thought to be the petrified tongues of dragons and snakes, or 'tongue stones'. They were carried as amulets and also used to divine poison. It seems that the threat of being poisoned was a general preoccupation in the medieval world.

Coco de Mer

The fabulously sensual-looking Coco de Mer is a 'fruit' that closely resembles a pair of female buttocks. It's the biggest seed in the plant kingdom, weighing up to a staggering 30 kilos. Until 1768, its origins were completely unknown and it was thought to grow on mythical trees at the bottom of the ocean. In fact the palms that bear them grow only on the Seychelles (which were uninhabited). The hollow shells of the germinated seeds would be carried on the tides and washed up on the shores of the Maldives, whence they were traded around the world as objects of curiosity – hence their other name, Maldive coconuts. Much like bezoars, they would be polished and mounted in precious metals, making enigmatic additions to a European cabinet of curiosity. They also found favour in the Islamic world and sometimes turn up in the form of

Dervish *kashkuls* or begging bowls, the exteriors ornately carved and decorated with copper mounts and handles. I recently saw a completely plain and unadorned example make over £6,000 at auction – not bad for a nut.

THE *ANTIQUES ROADSHOW*: A NATIONAL TREASURE

The British are obsessed by antiques. I use the word 'antiques' loosely because applied in its broadest sense it throws its comforting arm around a whole plethora of disciplines and genres ranging from Rembrandts to beer mats. The *Antiques Roadshow* is regarded by its adoring public as the Linus blanket of the television world, a national treasure, much copied but never bettered. In a digital world where TV audiences for live broadcasts are ever diminishing, it still regularly attracts over 6 million viewers. It's also among the longest running factual programmes on British television and airing its 36th series as this book goes to press.

I watched it in my teenage years, hooked from the word go, little knowing that I would one day be part of this esteemed institution. Having served on fifteen series and now working with my third presenter (Fiona Bruce, successor to Michael Aspel and Hugh Scully), I'm just beginning to feel like I have finished my apprenticeship – and it has been an honour. I'm what's known as a 'miscellaneous' specialist, which means I deal with just about every facet of the antiques and collectables world that you can imagine. This stems from my background as a general auctioneer – our queue is normally the longest!

So what is it about the *Roadshow* that has so captured the imagination of millions of viewers on cold winter Sunday evenings? The cynical among you might say that it's about greed and avarice. Those are strong words and although it's impossible to deny the lure of high-value discoveries, it has far more to do with passion and personal stories: both the passion of the specialist and the interests of the owner. The programmes reflect a mixture of values, which we as the go-betweens hope to put across to the viewers in a way that reflects our love for the subject, our empathy for the often poignant objects that we deal with and the high production values of the BBC.

If you've ever wondered how many people we've seen and how many objects we've handled, here are a few statistics to digest. As it currently stands, there have been 700 programmes made at 530 venues; eleven of those venues were in foreign countries, including Australia and Canada, where the *Roadshow* is immensely popular – in 2005 the visit to Australia prompted 25,000 ticket applications for just two shows! The format is also licensed in many countries, including places as diverse as America and Sweden, where they have their own versions.

Each show is visited by around 2,000–3,000 guests. It's estimated that specialists on the show have seen and valued around 9 million objects in total, of which approximately 20,000 have been filmed. No one is ever turned away on the day and it's a matter of pride that every person gets seen, no matter whether it's a humble cup and saucer or a valuable Fabergé brooch.

Protecting the spontaneity of the recordings is always of paramount importance. In these days of the internet, owners often can't resist finding out all they can before they arrive (we hate that) so it's doubly exciting when you find a genuinely surprising object that you can enthuse over.

I'm often asked things like 'Is it a fix? Someone told me you know what's coming in advance; how come you always have those big bits of furniture on the show?' We quite simply put an ad in the local paper close to where we are scheduled to film and wait for people to write in. After the office has received a hundred or so letters, we set off the week before with an advance party of two and visit as many people as we can. Having made some informed decisions, without giving any details away and often having to exercise great restraint, Pickfords pick up a few bulky pieces belonging to those who can't physically move the items themselves and we make a few appointments to get the cameras rolling in the morning before the queues filter through (since idle cameras cost money!).

A normal day involves filming around 50 objects and it's typical for a specialist such as myself to film between two and four pieces, although that very much depends on what turns up on the day.

So what, after all these years, are the objects that most stick in my mind? Napoleon's attaché case was pretty exciting; Marc Bolan's Gibson Flying V guitar was also impressive; a plate from Captain Scott's ship the *Terra Nova*, probably handled by the great man, was a very powerful object; and a torch made from an old OXO tin in the Second World War, presented by a glamorous lady in 1940s dress ... all part of a typical day's work on the *Antiques Roadshow*.

Before motorised lawnmowers with large pneumatic tyres floated gracefully over our lawns, horses or ponies generally did the job of pulling large mowing machines. In order to stop their hooves churning up the grass and ruining the surface, the Victorians had a novel idea – lawn boots. They come in two distinct varieties, leather boots ('bag type') or screw-on plate types. H. Pattison & Co. of Streatham, London, made over 30 different sizes in the late 19th century. Unlike most shoes, these naturally come in sets of four, and are, not surprisingly, a niche collectable.

WHAT'S IN A NAME?

Collecting is like eating peanuts, you just can't stop
—Anon

We all know that stamp collectors are called philatelists; in fact, if you were to try and summon up half a dozen names for collectors you'd probably just about manage it. One of my favourites is the name given to cigar band collectors – brandophilists. The current record holder is an American called Joe Hruby who is listed in the Guinness book of records as possessing 165,480 – although apparently that figure has long since been exceeded and now stands at over 220,000. His collection was accumulated over 70 years.

I've scouted around for a general title to cover my own multifarious collecting habits but can't really find a good term for a general collector. There are a few different names for hoarders, 'syllogomania' being one of them, but this usually refers to more extreme OCD (obsessive-compulsive disorder)-related cases. Perhaps a 'generalist' will suffice; however, if you collect a little bit 'off piste' then it's still possible to officially categorise yourself. Here are a few terms that might cover your particular collecting passion. This is by no means exhaustive but it might help you when you do your next crossword puzzle.

Ambulist – Walking sticks
Arctophilist – Teddy bears
Argyrotheocologist – Moneyboxes
Bibliophile – Books
Brolliologist – Umbrellas
Cagophilist – Keys
Cartomaniac – Maps
Conchologist – Shells
Cumyxaphilist or *Philluminist* – Matchboxes, matchbooks and labels
Deltiologist – Postcards
Digitabulist – Thimbles
Discophilist – Gramophone records
Exlibrist – Book plates
Fromologist – Cheese labels
Fusilatelist – Phone cards
Helixophilist – Corkscrews
Labeorphilist – Beer bottles
Lepidopterist – Butterflies and moths
Notaphilist – Banknotes
Numismatist – Coins
Palaeontologist – Fossils
Philographist – Autographs

Plangonologist – Dolls
Rhykenologist – Woodworking planes
Scripophilist – Bonds and share certificates
Sphragistiphist – Seals and signet rings
Tegestologist – Beer mats
Vecturist – Transport tokens
Vexillologist – Flags

> The suffixes 'ana' and 'ilia' are often used
> in the world of collecting to denote an
> assemblage of items related to a field. Such
> words can often seem trite: commonly
> used are 'tobacciana', 'railwayana',
> 'Americana', 'Victoriana' and 'automobilia'.

NAPOLEON'S PENIS

What you are now we used to be,
what we are now you will be.

—Inscription in the crypt of the Capuchin
monks in the church of Santa Maria della
Concezione dei Cappuccini, Rome

The collecting of human body parts is an area in which I
have a particular interest; it's an issue that raises all sorts
of moral questions, mainly because different cultures
and religions view the treatment of mortal remains in
vastly different ways. Strangely, our inherent curiosity
for the macabre tends to often override our judgement
in these matters. Religion and religious custom, in

particular, play an enormous role in our perception of what is acceptable.

My personal collection extends to a skull that we affectionately nicknamed Doris, a few reliquaries containing various parts of 'saints', some finger bones from a crypt and a cannibal's knife from the Sepik River region of New Guinea – it's fashioned from a human leg bone.

Hmmm, I hear you say, why would anyone want to own that? Firstly, it's important to look at the way these objects tie in historically and culturally. My first such acquisition was made in my early 20s and it helped to mould my thinking on the subject. I purchased a Tibetan skull adorned with silver appliqués and semi-precious stones. The cranium was hinged and lined with silver. I remember that first evening looking at it on the mantelpiece and thinking about the person it had once been. I'd made some enquiries on Tibetan views of death and had already come to the conclusion that the Buddhist notion 'that once the consciousness has left the body it doesn't matter how the body is handled or disposed of because in effect, it has just become an empty shell' was very sensible. I felt I had the justification for owning the skull and have since tended to apply Buddhist principles to my collecting habits.

However, it's a subject that has simmered away for ages, causing our museums to repatriate shrunken heads and other religious or culturally important body parts on a far less public scale than the controversy surrounding the Elgin marbles. (*See* Did Elgin Steal the Marbles? *page 55*.)

So where does Napoleon's penis fit into this? Well,

this is a salutary lesson on not making too many enemies and not being too infamous. It seems the more notorious you are, the more likely that people will want a piece of you – after you are dead. Taking a lock of hair is acceptable and a time-honoured measure of love and remembrance, but Napoleon had unfortunately left his physician, Dr Francesco Antommarchi, out of his will. On his death in 1821, an autopsy was carried out in the presence of seventeen worthies and officials. Gossip soon circulated about the 'souvenirs' that had been taken from Napoleon and his deathbed, including blood-stained sheets, hair, parts of his intestine and so on. Somehow, it seems, Napoleon's chaplain, the Abbé Ange Vignali, acquired his penis and it stayed with the family until 1916 when it was sold at auction to an unknown British collector.

In 1924 it was purchased by an American collector, A.S.W. Rosenbach, for £400. He used it as a conversation piece and even loaned it to the Museum of French Art in New York. It was again auctioned in 1969 but failed to sell and was acquired some eight years later at an auction in Paris by the eminent American urologist Dr John K. Lattimer for the equivalent of around $3,000. He died in 2007, leaving it to his daughter, who still owns it. Rumour has it that she has turned down an offer of $100,000 for the appendage.

For those curious as to its appearance, unfortunately no one is permitted to see it, but type 'Napoleon's penis' into YouTube and you can watch a four-minute film of the writer Tony Perrottet enjoying a private viewing. On behalf of Napoleon I feel obliged to point out that anything mummified shrinks, and so it can safely be assumed that it was at one time considerably larger than it is now.

> Albert Einstein's brain was removed shortly after his death in 1955 by the pathologist Thomas Stoltz Harvey. Whether or not it was removed with Einstein's prior permission has always been the subject of debate. It was preserved and divided up; some portions were given to other eminent pathologists, some parts were mounted for study and Harvey retained some sections himself. These were rediscovered in 1978, still in Harvey's possession, and caused a media frenzy. It's unlikely that any will ever be sold, but the sale in 2010 of an X-ray of Einstein's brain, taken in 1945, encourages speculation about how much they could, in theory, realise; the X-ray sold for £24,000.

COINING IT

Collecting is an infection which is more intractable than any virus and from which there is no inoculation and no immunity
—Arthur Sackler

The bulk of the world's most expensive coins are American. In many ways that's hardly surprising as virtually all 'top tens' seem to be based around the propensity for the American market to collect bigger and better, particularly with home-grown material. Therefore, I have to make an apology to British readers for high values mostly being quoted in dollars, but whatever the currency, there's no denying that rarity and history combine to produce some startling effects. Here are a few of the largest prices paid to date for these numismatic gems:

The 'Flowing Hair' dollar was the first dollar coin issued by the United States Federal Government. It was minted in 1794 and 1795 and an example was sold in 2005 for $7.85 million. Hot on its heels is the fabled 1933 Saint-Gaudens 'Double Eagle', a 90 per cent pure gold coin first minted in 1849 and sold in 2002 for $7.59 million. (Most were melted down before circulation.) The 1804 silver dollar has a complicated history and was mostly produced in diplomatic presentation sets, but an example known as the 'Watters-Childs' specimen – one of only fifteen known – raised $4.14 million in 1999. Breaking the mould slightly was the sale of the monster 20kg Canadian 'Maple Leaf'. With a $1 million face value the 53cm coin was made by the Canadian Royal Mint as a publicity tool. Only one was struck, and this was auctioned as part of the insolvency sale of an investment group. It made €3.27 million. Sold recently in 2013 is the 'Liberty Head' nickel. Minted in 1913, this five cent coin is extremely rare and was sold for $3.7 million. (A mint example would make far more.) Top of the English tree is the beautiful Edward III gold 'Double Leopard' of 1344. Only three are known to exist. One was sold in 2006 by Spink of London for £460,000.

Two pieces of advice: don't for a moment think that similar coins are likely to appear in your loose change; and beware, there are quite a few fakes around.

A GHOST STORY

The idea that a building might act as a type of 'tape recorder' has long been a subject of great conjecture. Do ghosts really exist? Do objects have the power to memorise people and events? However sceptical you are, the very foundation of my belief was challenged by an event many years ago.

We had cleared a house, the contents of which had come in to the auction rooms ready to be sorted for sale. Part of the contents comprised of a large trunk full of paperwork and letters. The letters were tied in small bundles with fine blue ribbon, still in their original envelopes and bearing postmarks from the 1920s. Several of us untied and looked at some of the missives and it very soon became apparent that they were a very poignant and sensitive collection of love letters sent between two women. We jokingly read some small passages aloud and no doubt passed some flippant remarks concerning their sexuality in a different epoch and how this may have been successfully effected at the time. At the end we were left with a dilemma: how do you sell something so personal, let alone put a value on it?

Two days later a lady came into the office. I handled an over-the-counter valuation for her and she left some items for sale. I remember being struck by an air of solemnity. She had a slightly tearful look but I didn't think much else of it. However, the next day she came back. On this occasion she looked more tearful and somewhat perturbed. She asked if I remembered her from yesterday and I replied in the affirmative.

'I had to come back,' she said, 'I took someone home with me yesterday.'

I looked at her quizzically, not at all sure what she meant.

'You looked at some letters recently.'

The hairs rose on the back of my neck and my eyes widened.

'They were tied with blue ribbon. The lady that they belonged to has been standing at the end of my bed all night and I've brought her back.'

There was no way she could possibly have known.

PUNCH AND JOAN

Some years ago there was a campaign to try and tone down the violence at seaside Punch and Judy shows. Mr Punch's misogynistic and violent tendencies were not considered a good role model for youngsters. However, rather like a similar campaign to ban *Tom and Jerry* cartoons, it appears to have found little success; you only have to see the hordes of children on the beach, laughing heartily at Mr Punch's flagrant wife-beating and death by crocodile, to realise that Punch and Judy are enshrined in our culture.

Despite this, Punch and Judy do not originate from British shores; they are in fact Italian and come from the 16th-century tradition of *commedia dell'arte*. Punch's name is a corruption of *Pulcinella*, who was the personification of the Lord of Misrule.

The character was first recorded as being seen in England on 9 May 1662, now officially Mr Punch's birthday.

Samuel Pepys records such a show in his diary, performed by Pietro Gimonde in Covent Garden. There are many characters in Punch and Judy shows, including the baby, the constable and the doctor, but Judy, Punch's long-suffering wife, was originally called Joan.

The popularity of the show in the 18th and 19th centuries spawned a plethora of related objects. Collectors can choose from cast-iron doorstops, often colourfully painted (and faked) cast-iron moneyboxes, brass nutcrackers with opposing figures forming the 'arms', silver menu holders, bronze figures and garden statuary. Royal Doulton made a figure called 'Punch and Judy Man' (catalogue number HN 2765) and representations in ceramic, literary form and of course puppets abound. Punch's jester's hat, hunchback and hooked nose are his characteristic traits.

Mr Punch, from a 19th-century etching by George Cruikshank

IS IT POSSIBLE TO DIE OF NOSTALGIA?

They (psychologists) say that anything that either arouses
or relaxes or induces fantasies can lead to addiction.
Collecting does all three, and so is especially addictive
—Harry Beran

The word 'nostalgia' is an ancient derivative coined from the Greek *nóstos* for 'homecoming' and álgos for 'pain' or 'ache', so it literally means 'homesick'. We tend to associate the word with pleasurable experiences plucked from our rose-tinted memories, triggering a combination of emotions based on everything from your favourite sweets to the toys played with in childhood.

We're all guilty of reminiscing about bygone eras, vintage television shows, steam travel, clothing, etc. It's an intrinsic element of our make-up: we hanker for the enjoyable elements of our past and we associate them with strong sensory markers such as smell, touch and music.

It's a rather intangible side of human nature that has largely confounded the scientific community over the centuries. What actually is nostalgia? What is certain is that the meaning of nostalgia has changed considerably over the centuries; it was once considered a serious medical condition and there are various references littered through history that mention the debilitating effects of a bad bout of nostalgia on groups such as soldiers and sailors. In essence, this homesickness or 'melancholy' was considered a potential killer and symptoms would be manifested in fevers or, more likely, serious states of depression (a modern definition), leading to desertion and suicide. In the 18th century it was even thought that the very essence of nostalgia was located in a 'nostalgic bone'.

One facet of this 'malady', in the modern sense of the word, is that it is not limited to happy memories but can also foster strong feelings of sadness or sorrow – a natural reaction to something that might be lost.

By the late 19th century the idea of nostalgia as a medical condition had all but died out. Gradually, the power of nostalgia has turned into a commercially exploitable concept that draws upon our desperate desire to reinvent and relive the past. We see it in every facet of life, from the food we eat to the cars we drive. The term 'retro' litters our language in a constant barrage of recycled and upcycled ideas and designs.

Most importantly of all, and the main point of this little etymological jaunt, is that nostalgia has evolved into a raison d'être; it is one of the most powerful stimuli in our unfathomable neurological desire to collect.

A personal top ten of nostalgic toys

1. Corgi James Bond Aston Martin DB5, featured in the film *Goldfinger*, issued 1965. Over 3 million of the original version were sold.

2. Action Man. Launched in 1966 by Palitoy, with vintage examples and accessories now highly collectable.

3. Johnny Seven O.M.A. (One Man Army) machine gun made by Deluxe Reading under the brand Topper Toys; the top-selling boys' toy of 1964.

4. 1967 Scalextric special edition James Bond slot car set, featuring the Aston Martin DB5 with working ejector seat.

5. Lady Penelope's FAB1 Rolls-Royce from the series *Thunderbirds*, made by Meccano Ltd under the Dinky brand name and issued in 1967.

6. Rock 'em Sock 'em Robots by Marx. Issued in 1964, these plastic boxing robots in a ring have become pop-culture cult classics.

7. Lego was invented in 1949 by Dane Ole Kirk Christiansen. It is the best-selling construction toy in the world with a current average manufacturing output of about 36 billion bricks per year.

8. The Etch-a-Sketch was invented by a Frenchman called André Cassagnes in the late 1950s. It came on to the market in 1960 and was highly successful. It's considered a cult toy and used by adults, artists and children alike.

9. Meccano was invented in 1901 by Frank Hornby of Hornby trains fame. This metal bolt-together construction toy is one of the iconic toys of the 20th century. Both educational and creative, it's a toy that garners great nostalgia. It is sadly less popular these days but much collected in its vintage form.

10. Monopoly (*see* A Complete Monopoly, *page 168*), the world's best-selling board game at around 250 million units sold.

DROP-DEAD GORGEOUS

We live in an age rife with health and safety controls. Some of these regulations seem draconian and as our appetite for litigation increases, employers and manufacturers are increasingly cautious of becoming embroiled in costly cases. However, it's interesting to note that there are many objects seen as desirable within the world of antiques and collectables that were manufactured prior to the existence of any protective legislation. Some posed a great risk to the people who worked with them at the time and some can still pose something of a risk now. Far be it from me to scaremonger but here are few areas worth considering.

Arsenic

Arsenic (As) is one of the most commonly occurring chemical elements on the planet and one of the most highly toxic. It has also historically been one of the most useful, providing a whole range of applications, from the hardening of alloys to medical uses; from pesticides, preservatives and poisons to taxidermy, embalming and colouring. Arsenic pills were even legitimately sold as an aid to the complexion and it was said that 'arsenic eaters' were always recognisable by their youthful glowing looks (up until it killed them, that is!). Arsenic pervaded virtually every strand of life and was readily available, sold over the counter by many general grocers without any form of control or safeguard for separating it from foodstuffs or other goods.

Until methods of detection were invented in the 19th century, beginning with the Marsh test in 1836, arsenic was also the favoured clandestine method for murdering people. Slowly and surely, it could be administered in small doses, the effects most likely taken for some disease such as consumption, leading to a slow and agonising death.

Deliberate poisonings aside, the misuse of arsenic accounted for much death and suffering in the 19th century and there are countless documented cases of families being poisoned by its accidental inclusion in cooking, often when it was mistaken for a foodstuff by servants, it having been stored in reused food containers in proximity to the kitchen for use as rat poison.

However, its legitimate use in industrial and domestic situations was also a major hazard, one of which most people were simply not aware.

It was used as an ingredient in the compound Scheele's green, a colouring that was used to dye everything from sweets to fabrics, wallpaper and absinthe. The stories of its toxic capabilities abound, with mass poisonings caused by careless confectioners, greedy businessmen – who substituted it for more expensive elements in food production – and careless (or ambivalent) employers whose workers had little choice but to earn money at the expense of their health and life expectancy.

In many places of employment, particularly in industries such as the artificial flower business so beloved of Victorian ladies, the workers were constantly exposed in their long working days to the arsenical dust from agents such as Scheele's green. Consequently, they would ride a roller coaster of ill health and sometimes death.

The same colours were used in the textile industry, leading to exposure for both the workers and the wearers. The popular use of emerald green in the Victorian period led to a problem that would ultimately lead to the expression 'drop-dead gorgeous', in reference to the beautiful women in their ballgowns, swirling in clouds of arsenical dust, poisoning both themselves and their suitors.

Uranium

I can remember when we filmed an annual *Children's Antiques Roadshow*. We had a wonderful stunt that highlighted the surprises of collecting certain 'contaminated' objects. We had a Geiger counter and we would wait expectantly for a family to arrive with some 'uranium' glass. The glass is coloured with uranium oxide and fluoresces brightly under ultraviolet light; it also produces a heightened reaction when exposed to the Geiger counter. Some forms, known commonly as Vaseline glass and Depression glass are commonly collected and popular with the American market. In fact, they rarely register much higher than background radiation, but nevertheless are not recommended for eating off!

Radium

In a similar vein are the glow-in-the dark watch dials, which up until the 1950s were commonly painted with paint containing radium. These watches, unlike modern versions with non-radioactive light-charged numerals, were painted with a mixture of radium and zinc sulphide. The zinc sulphide glows brightly when hit by the radium and even though the painted numerals on an old watch may have decayed to a yellowish, non-luminous state, the worn-out zinc is still bombarded with radium that has a half-life of 1,600 years! The hazards faced by the workers who produced these dials have become enshrined in the folklore of dangerous collectables, their lives shortened by licking the cancerous paintbrushes that they worked with every day.

Collectors of old military watches (where such dials are often found), are advised to wear them in moderation, not in bed, and not to continually leave them on the bedside table. The greatest hazard is the potential inhalation of broken-up particles from the dials, which can cause cancerous tumours on the lungs.

Other potentially hazardous areas can include possible exposure to pathogens in old medical and veterinary equipment; dangerous pigments used on grave goods such as red lead and cinnabar; poisonous seeds used in ethnographic decoration on textiles and jewellery; poison on old edged weapons and darts; exposure to lead and mercury in paints, old instruments, barometers, etc.; unstable antique ammunition; and asbestos in old electrical items, to name but a few. Did you think collecting was a safe pastime? Don't worry, on the whole, it is.

A HISTORY OF -ISMS

The history of art is the history of revivals
—Samuel Butler

The '-ism' is a particularly important aspect of the art world. In discussing them we are basically looking at the history of art movements, so if you are rusty on your '-isms' then you won't be able to show a fully informed knowledge of art history.

An art movement is basically defined as a 'style or tendency' cemented by a 'common philosophy' and observed by a group of artists over a particular period. Some art movements were very short lived; others, such as Romanticism, lasted over a hundred years, and were massively influential, their ideals migrating into literature, music and architecture.

The idea of art movements is mainly a 19th- and 20th-century phenomenon. In pursuit of the avant-garde, the idea of creating a movement was to some extent a self-promoting, egotistical fad. Write a manifesto, think of an '-ism', gather a few absinthe-swigging artist friends together and Bob's your uncle! Simplistic perhaps but not altogether untrue.

Art movements don't all end in '-ism' so the list below does not pretend to be exhaustive in terms of art history. It does however provide a useful overview of some of the key movements of the past few hundred years.

Mannerism c.1520–early 17th century
Neoclassicism c.1750–1800

19th century
Cloisonnism c.1888–1900s
Divisionism c.1880s–1910s
Expressionism c.1890s–1930s
Impressionism 1860s–1920s
Modernism 1860s–present
Naturalism
Norwegian Romantic Nationalism c.1840–1867
Orientalism

Pointillism
Realism
Spanish Eclecticism
Symbolism
Synthetism
Tonalism

20th century
1900–1918
American Realism
Analytic Cubism c.1909–1912
Constructivism c.1920–1922; 1920s–1940s
Cubism c.1906–1919
Cubo-Futurism c.1912–1918
Czech Cubism c.1910–1914
Dadaism c.1916
Fauvism c.1900–1910
Futurism c.1909–1916
Luminism c.1900s–1930s
Modernism c.1860s–present
Orphism c.1910–1913
Purism c.1917–1930s
Rayonism
Suprematism formed c.1915–16
Synchromism founded 1912
Synthetic Cubism c.1912–1919
Vorticism founded 1914

1918–1945
Magic Realism
Neo-Romanticism

Precisionism c.1918–1940s
Religionism c.1930s–1940s
Socialist Realism
Surrealism c.1920s–1960s

1945–1965
Abstract Expressionism
Lettrism
New Brutalism
Tachism

1965–2000
Abstract Illusionism
Classical Realism
Late Modernism
Massurrealism
Minimalism
Neo-Expressionism
Postminimalism
Postmodernism
Photorealism

21st century
Altermodernism
Hyperrealism
Intentism
Metamodernism
Neo-Minimalism
Post-Postmodernism
Remodernism

LOOKING GLASS

Glass – one of the most versatile materials ever invented. Its applications are myriad and yet we generally take it for granted. Its ingredients are basic: silica, sodium oxide and lime. Used for centuries in basic products such as drinking vessels, bottles, window glass and packaging, its incredible versatility makes it an ideal material for both humble and luxurious objects. From its ancient origins to modern times, the evolution of glass has been adapted to our technological and domestic needs; but who first discovered its secret?

Glass existed long before its 'invention'. It occurs in several natural forms: obsidian or volcanic glass has been used since prehistoric times; knapped like flint, glass tools, including arrow heads and blades, have been in existence for millennia and were a favourite of the Maya. Fulgurites are solidified hollow tubes of molten silica formed by lightning strikes – a basic form of glass. And tektites are a natural form of glass formed by meteor impacts (*see* Mythical Objects, *page 5*).

According to the Roman historian Pliny the Elder, the Phoenicians accidentally discovered glass some 5,000 years BC. Georgius Agricola in *De re metallica* quotes a similar tale of discovery:

> The tradition is that a merchant ship laden with nitrum [ammonium nitrate] being moored at this place, the merchants were preparing their meal on the beach, and not having stones to prop up their pots, they used lumps of nitrum from the ship, which fused and mixed

with the sands of the shore, and there flowed streams
of a new translucent liquid, and thus was the origin of
glass.

Interestingly, the earliest known forms of glass are
beads dating from some 3,000 years before the birth of
Christ, although it is thought that these might even be
the accidental slag-based by-products of metalworking.
Glass production was certainly practised extensively by
the Greeks and Egyptians in the 15th century BC but
given the archaeological evidence for the shipping of
glass ingots, it seems likely that the secrets of making it
were closely guarded, leaving the raw glass to be worked
by other cultures in its cold state using mechanical
techniques.

Glass was also formed as ceramic glazes. We rarely
stop to consider the proximity of these to the type of glass
that we know today. Glazes are thought to have been in
use as early as the 8th or 9th century BC, perhaps even
earlier, and various cultures and civilisations such as the
Egyptians, Chinese and Mesopotamians developed their
own forms. Ancient glazing recipes include ash mixed
with sand and soda mixed with sand – the basic constituents of glass. However, 'true' glazing came after the
invention of glass. The Romans were certainly using a lead
oxide and sand glaze by the 1st century BC. The earliest
known instructions for making glass come from cuneiform
tablets, circa 650BC, discovered in the library of the Assyrian king Ashurbanipal.

As to the skill of ancient glassmakers, we can hardly
dispute their ability to create everything from the most

humble of objects to some of the greatest and revered works of art in our most important institutions: the so-called Portland Vase, a Roman cameo masterpiece thought to date from around AD5–25, is undoubtedly one of the greatest treasures of the British Museum and a highly influential object in art history, with a wonderfully intriguing history to boot.

Innovation in glass production has continued over the millennia; a few paragraphs can do its history little justice, but from the advent of crown glass for windows produced by the French in the early 14th century to the skill of modern Scandinavian and Italian designers – via the industrial mass-production of Pilkington 'float' glass in the 1950s, finely executed 16th- and 17th-century Venetian glass and the originality of Lalique – glass is and will continue to be a fascinating medium for the collector.

Taken from a good old 15th-century root, the colloquial term 'friggers' was used to describe the 'spare-time' output of glassmakers. These fripperies, particularly from the Victorian period, include glass walking canes, elaborate ships under glass domes and various other flights of fancy. Detractors argue that glassmakers had very little spare time and that the glass they used to make such things was not 'left over' – the glass itself was far too valuable to contemplate wasting. However, the word persists in relatively common usage.

THE LANGUAGE OF JEWELLERY

There are many things in life that will catch your eye,
but only a few will catch your heart ... pursue those
—Anon

'A diamond is forever' – it's a phrase we all know and perhaps one of the most successful advertising campaigns of the 20th century, a clever marketing ploy invented for De Beers by a Madison Avenue advertising person to emphasise the eternal sentiment of love in a jewel that is, strangely enough, one of the most commonly occurring gemstones on the planet.

The Greeks believed that diamonds were hardened dewdrops and regarded them as emblems of eternal love and purity. Such ancient sentiments reinforce the notion of gems having a meaning way beyond their decorative value. This is a time-honoured notion that has imbued gems and subsequently jewellery as a whole with a spiritual, mystical and highly emotional nuance that surpasses mere notions of adornment.

Although we often give jewellery for romantic and sentimental reasons, we seem to be less in tune with some of the meanings traditionally attached; here's some explanation and interpretation that may help you to plan your next Valentine's Day present with just a little more aplomb than usual.

Acrostic jewellery
Acrostic jewellery is something that you may not have heard of. Acrostic is a form of writing, perhaps poetry,

where a first letter, syllable or even a word can be taken to form another meaning – a hidden meaning. The idea of making jewellery in this way seems to have originated in France in the early 19th century. Of course, the notion of hiding meaning or creating a 'language of love' was not new: when, in 1527, Anne Boleyn caved in to Henry's advances, she sent him a small symbolic jewel depicting a maiden in a ship being tossed around in a stormy sea. Although no longer in existence, the jewel is recorded and we know that it would have sent a clear message to Henry that Anne desired his protection from the storms of life and that the best way to do that was to marry her. As it turned out, he cut off her head!

The enthusiasm for acrostic jewellery was transmitted to England from the French capital; the inventor, as appears to be well documented, was Jean-Baptiste Mellerio, ex-jeweller to Marie Antoinette and subsequently patronised by the Empress Josephine. The jewellery was retailed at the House of Mellerio *dits* Meller (which incidentally is still in business). Mellerio devised an alphabet of gems with which to spell out various sentiments, which of course worked well in the highly romantic 'Gallic' language. Using French names for gems, and sometimes old-fashioned names or the colours of the stones to fudge some of the less utilised letters of the alphabet, words or phrases such as *J'adore* ('I love you') would be spelt out using (in this case) jacinth (*jacinte*), amethyst (*améthyste*), diamond (*diamante*), opal (*opale*), ruby (*rubis*) and emerald (*émeraud*).

Despite the fact that Britain was at war with France, French was still regarded as the language of the educated upper classes and so the romantic associations of popularly used words such as *souvenir* (remembrance) and *amitié* (friendship) were easily transposed to Britain where the popularity for such jewellery quickly blossomed. One of the most common English acrostic pieces is for the word *Regard* using ruby, emerald, garnet, amethyst, ruby and diamond.

A Amethyst Agate Aquamarine	B Beryl	C Citrine Coral Carnelian	D Diamond
E Emerald	G Garnet	H Hyalite Hematite	I Iolite Iris
J Jasper Jet Jacinth (Red Zircon)	L Lapis	M Malachite	N Natrolite Nephrite (Jade)
O Opal Onyx	P Peridot (Olivine) Pearl	Q Quartz	R Ruby
S Sapphire	T Topaz Turquoise	U Unakite	V Vermeil (Garnet)

Language of flowers

Also becoming popular in the 19th century, arising from a fashionable preoccupation with botany, were naturalistic pieces based on the 'language of flowers'. This trend can be seen mainly in Victorian and Edwardian jewellery. Forget-me-nots were a common motif, set with seed pearls and turquoise denoting love, purity, friendship and peace and often found on lockets and brooches. Daisies denoted innocence, ivy marriage.

The meaning of some symbols was understandably personal to lovers and friends, so by the very nature of the subject it was not always desirable that other people could immediately decipher the meaning of the jewels that one was wearing. Jewellers therefore had to strike a balance between conveying the message and not making it too obvious.

All of this is an area sadly overlooked by most modern jewellery buyers, who seem to have reverted to a focus on pure adornment rather than a combination of adornment and sentiment. Perhaps the stage is set for a return to good old-fashioned romanticism.

> One of my favourite examples of symbolism in jewellery is the Ouroboros, an ancient symbol of a serpent or dragon devouring its own tail, first seen in Egypt in the 14th century BC and a strong representation of constancy, longevity and perpetual recreation. It is often found manifested in jewellery as a bracelet or as a border on brooches and lockets.

TRETCHIKOFF – KING OF KITSCH?

You need a big ego to be an artist
—Damien Hirst

In my view, kitsch is the antidote to all that is serious in the world of antiques and collecting. No matter how focused and obsessed you are about a subject you should always reserve a little bit of space for an object or a piece of art that defies all notions of 'good taste'. Indeed, some kitsch is so gaudy that it transcends categorisation as 'bad taste' and becomes 'good taste' by default. I favour glow-in-the-dark religious souvenirs or Pierre et Gilles lenticular pictures – you can't beat a good bit of vintage Catholic kitsch.

The word apparently originates from the late 19th-century art markets of Munich, where it was used to describe cheap pictures. 'Kitsch' may well have derived from the German verb *verkitschen*, meaning 'to make cheap', or it may be a derivation of the Russian *keetcheet-sya*, meaning 'to be haughty and puffed up'.

The University of Chicago *Theories of Media* word glossary describes kitsch as a 'negative product ... a source of sheer entertainment in opposition to the elevated perception generated by high art.' In essence, this is the very purpose of kitsch. Their highly academic analysis of kitsch and the human condition makes interesting reading but in essence boils down to something very simple: kitsch essentially 'rivals reality while simultaneously imitating its effects'. While there is a difference between ironic items that are specifically designed for the collectors' market and those accidental objects such as resin tourist souvenirs of the Coliseum liberally sprinkled with purple glitter, both are capable of transcending international notions of taste and popular appeal.

Indeed, art itself continually pays homage to the genre, with artists such as Damien Hirst and Jeff Koons taking its exploitation to new heights. However, it was the sale in 2013 of an iconic image that prompted this little jaunt through the world of light-up Eiffel Towers and Mexican Day of the Dead shopping bags. 'Chinese Girl', sometimes known as 'The Green Lady', is without doubt one of the best-known images in the world and has been reproduced millions of times since it was painted in the 1950s by the Siberian-born artist Vladimir Tretchikoff. He passed away in Cape Town in 2006 at the age of 92 and was never happy with the kitsch label being applied to his work. However, 'Chinese Girl' along with other works by Tretchikoff such as 'The Dying Swan' and 'Blue Monday' have come to symbolise mainstream kitsch and Tretchikoff's successful style has spawned thousands of imitators. The fact that it sold at auction for just short of a million pounds and was bought by the multi-billionaire jeweller and businessman Laurence Graff genuinely lends weight to the notion that kitsch has grown up.

A CATALOGUE OF ERRORS

Painting is easy when you don't know how, but very difficult when you do
—Edgar Degas

Apparently, auctioneering falls within the top ten most stressful occupations. I can testify to the intensity of relentlessly gaining goods for sale and continuously working towards catalogue deadlines with 2,000 lot sales sapping your last ounce of energy as you beaver away well into the night. Of course, mistakes are bound to happen and the human chain required to input some barely legible late-night cataloguing descriptions can lead to some humorous faux pas in the finished glossy production. So I decided to collate a few amusing ones that have slipped through the net, despite all the proofreading and the arrival of computer spellcheckers.

Just the other day I was waiting for a lot to be sold; the auctioneer was motoring along, giving a few words of the description before asking for bids. The pronouncement of 'Lot 1597, Stag in a Bag', was followed by an audible titter among the audience as the catalogue error was hastily but light-heartedly corrected to a more typical Victorian title – 'Stag in a Bog'.

Some of the best ones need a little bit of deciphering. A rather funny example was recounted to me by a friend in the picture trade, who noticed that a painting of a shepherd with his faithful sheepdog lying at his feet was attributed to the artist Ebenezer Newman Downard. In fact, the dog was dead and the painting was entitled 'END'! On a more basic level I was amused to see that two lovely shire horses had been subjected to late-night dyslexia turning them into 'shite horses', which must have been embarrassing for the auction house concerned as each vendor is generally sent a catalogue prior to the sale.

For years, the Old Masters department in a certain auction house often attributed unknown Dutch genre pictures to a little-known artist called Hertz Van Rentall, until the ruse was eventually spotted by a journalist. The name 'Eneret' also seemed to pop up frequently, particularly in the field of sculpture and bronze. It took a particular Dane who works in the art and auction world to point out to the major houses that 'eneret' translates as 'copyright'.

Picture descriptions are often open to some personal interpretation; those that do not fit the typical stock of readily useable titles such as 'Highland Cattle', can be left to the cataloguer's creative side. However, one such incident whereby a large oil of a lady handing some gold coins to a young boy was given the title 'Passing the Hard Ecu' led to the furious vendor withdrawing the picture from the sale altogether!

STATE OF PLAY

The idea that a print might change over time seems like a strange idea but it's something that's quite common in the world of antique prints where the 'state' of an image may be altered over time for several reasons. Be it from a woodblock, a copper plate or a stone block, the artist might make a print to check on the progress of the plate; this is usually called a proof impression. A plate that is then heavily used and becomes worn might need to be reworked in order to refresh it. Other reasons might be even more drastic with faces or scenes being totally altered for use in different publications or situations.

To give an example, the 1515 woodcut of Albrecht Dürer's famous Rhinoceros is referred to as 'first state'. Between 4,000 and 5,000 are estimated to have been printed in Dürer's lifetime. There were many other editions printed after his death but this version, identifiable by the five lines of script above the image, is naturally the most valuable. A first-state print was sold in New York in January 2013 by Christie's for a record-breaking $866,500.

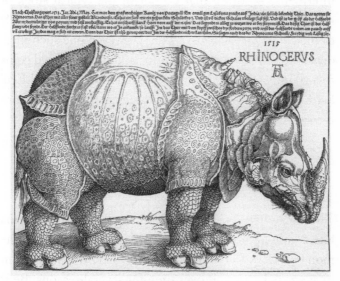

Dürer's Rhinoceros

The world's oldest surviving printed book is thought to be the Diamond Sutra, a Buddhist holy text dated AD868. It was copied by a man called Wong Jei in May of that year and was discovered in 1907 in a walled-up cave in Dunhuang, north-west China by the explorer Sir Marc Aurel Stein. This book (or scroll) predates moveable type in Europe by hundreds of years.

ULFBERHTS, CHANEL HANDBAGS, PATENTS AND COPYRIGHT

We all know how prevalent is the copying and counterfeiting of designs, goods and ideas. Everything from jeans to wristwatches and handbags to cigarettes constantly flood the market, in breach of and with scant regard for the systems that are set up to protect brands, customer safety and quality. This is not a new phenomenon: since ancient times counterfeiting and copying has been rife and even Pliny the Elder moaned about the counterfeit wine and bronzes that were for sale in the markets of Rome.

Even the Vikings weren't immune. The Ulfberht was the favoured sword of wealthy Viking warriors, a superior fighting weapon fashioned from crucible steel and technologically beyond the capabilities of any known Viking foundries. Made between AD800 and 1100, the blades were signed '+vlfberh+t' and were undoubtedly the result of traded Eastern technology or raw materials. To this day, no archaeological evidence for this elusive foundry has been found within the Viking realm. But guess what: there are fakes bearing the Ulfberht signature; inferior quality to the real McCoy but probably sold 'cut price' to some label-conscious warriors. Apparently, a scientific metallurgical analysis has shown that swords bearing the name '+vlfberht+' (the cross is in a different place) are inferior steel. So just like a knock-off Chanel handbag with a badly riveted strap, it seems that a half-price Ulfberht was highly likely to leave you wishing you hadn't gone for the cheaper alternative!

Copyright in literature was not a great issue until the invention of the printing press; prior to this, manuscripts were hand-copied, an expensive and laborious process, meaning few were actually produced. In England, the Stationers' Company had exercised a controlling register of legally published books since the 16th century but this monopoly was to end in 1694 when a new statute was set up. Known as the Statute of Anne, after Queen Anne, it gave publishers of books fourteen years' protection; as the first copyright statute, it changed the whole face of publishing, effectively doing away with the system that stifled any publications not lawfully sanctioned, and making printed material more readily available to the masses.

So, attempts to protect creative rights are also nothing new, but until forms of control started to be implemented that afforded some form of protection to inventors, writers and artists, backed by strong legal recourse, it was open season for the unscrupulous rivals of hard-working producers to copy products and marks and publications. It is interesting to note that perhaps only about one in twenty pieces of 19th-century porcelain that I've handled bearing the famous crossed swords mark of Meissen are actually by Meissen. The others are just pale imitations but painted with the same or very similar marks. It's a common trait in the 19th-century ceramics industry and something that is still all too widespread as Eastern producers openly flout European copyright rules in many aspects of the modern market.

If you collect antique ceramics and glass it is not uncommon to come across some early forms of design copyright and patent registration marks printed or moulded on to objects. An 1842 act initiated a system of marking various classes of objects with a diamond- or kite-shaped mark. This verified that the design had been registered in Britain with the patent office, giving three years' copyright protection. This went through two cycles until it was replaced in 1883 with the Patents, Designs & Trademarks Act, which used a far simpler system of design registration numbers called 'Rd' numbers. These give the date for which the design of an item was registered, although objects bearing these numbers may well have been produced for some years afterwards, depending on their success. I carry around a list of the numbers in my wallet for quick reference; the ledgers with all the details are held in the National Archives and it is possible to view or apply online for copies of the original entries. Sadly, some have been lost.

Opposite is the key for working out a diamond mark, followed by the far easier table of Rd numbers on page 52.

Another useful pointer for the dating of objects came with the passing of the McKinley Tariff Act of 1891, which required all goods imported into the United States to be marked with their country of origin. The addition of the word 'England' was used from that date until about 1909, and then 'Made in England' until gradually superseded by 'Made in Britain'.

Design registration kite marks

1842–1867
The letter or number at each vertex of the diamond indicates either a component of the date or the parcel number. The roman numeral at the top indicates the class of goods.

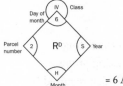 = 10 September 1848

Year
1842 X; 1843 H; 1844 C; 1845 A; 1846 I; 1847 F; 1848 U; 1849 S; 1850 V; 1851 P; 1852 D; 1853 Y; 1854 J; 1855 E; 1856 L; 1857 K; 1858 B; 1859 M; 1860 Z; 1861 R; 1862 O; 1863 G; 1864 N; 1865 W; 1866 Q; 1867 T

Month
January C; February G; March W; April H; May E; June M; July I; August R; September D*; October B; November K; December A**

* Except for 1–19 September 1957, when R was used
** Except for December 1960, when K was used

1868–1883
In this cycle, the parcel number and components of the date are at different points of the diamond.

= 6 April 1875

Year
1868 X; 1869 H; 1870 C; 1871 A; 1872 I; 1873 F; 1874 U; 1875 S; 1876 V; 1877 P; 1878 D*; 1879 Y; 1880 J; 1881 E; 1882 L; 1883 K

* Except for 1–6 March 1878, when W was used

Month
January C; February G; March W*; April H; May E; June M; July I; August R; September D; October B; November K; December A

* Except for 1–6 March 1878, when G was used

Rd numbers

1884–1885	1–19755	19755	1925–1926	710165–718056	7891
1886–1886	19756–40479	20723	1926–1927	718057–726329	8272
1886–1887	40480–64519	20439	1927–1928	726330–734369	8039
1887–1888	64520–90482	25962	1928–1929	734370–742724	8354
1888–1889	90483–116647	26164	1929–1930	742725–751159	8434
1889–1890	116648–141272	24624	1930–1931	751160–760582	9422
1890–1891	141273–163766	22493	1931–1932	760583–769669	9086
1891–1892	163767–185712	21945	1932–1933	769670–779291	9621
1892–1893	185713–205239	19526	1933–1934	779292–789018	9726
1893–1894	205240–224719	19479	1934–1935	789019–799096	10077
1894–1895	224720–246974	22254	1935–1936	799097–808793	9696
1895–1896	246975–268391	21416	1936–1937	808794–817292	8498
1896–1897	268392–291240	22848	1937–1938	817293–825230	7937
1897–1898	291241–311657	20416	1938–1939	825231–832609	7378
1898–1899	311658–331706	20048	1939–1940	832610–837519	4909
1899–1900	331707–351201	19494	1940–1941	837520–838589	1069
1900–1901	351202–368153	16951	1941–1942	838590–839229	639
1901–1902	368154–385179	17025	1942–1943	839230–839979	749
1902–1903	385180–403199	18019	1943–1944	839980–841039	1059
1903–1904	403200–424399	21199	1944–1945	841040–842669	1629
1904–1905	424400–447799	23399	1945–1946	842670–845549	2879
1905–1906	447800–471859	24059	1946–1947	845550–849729	4179
1906–1907	471860–493899	22039	1947–1948	849730–853259	3529
1907–1908	493900–518639	24739	1948–1949	853260–856998	3738
1908–1909	518640–535169	16529	1949–1950	856999–860853	3854
1909–1910	535170–551999	16829	1950–1951	860854–863969	3115
1910–1911	552000–574816	22816	1951–1952	863970–866279	2309
1911–1912	574817–594194	19377	1952–1953	866280–869299	3019
1912–1913	594195–612430	18235	1953–1954	869300–872530	3230
1913–1914	612431–630189	17758	1954–1955	872531–876066	3535
1914–1915	630190–644934	14744	1955–1956	876067–879281	3214
1915–1916	644935–653520	8585	1956–1957	879282–882948	3666
1916–1917	653521–658987	5466	1957–1958	882949–887078	4129
1917–1918	658988–662871	3883	1958–1959	887079–891664	4585
1918–1919	662872–666127	3255	1959–1960	891665–894999	3334
1919–1920	666128–673749	7621	1960–1961	895000–899913	4913
1920–1921	673750–680146	6396	1961–1962	899914–904637	4723
1921–1922	680147–687143	6996	1962–1963	904638–909363	4725
1922–1923	687144–694998	7854	1963–1964	903664–914535	5171
1923–1924	694999–702670	7671	1964–1965	914536–919607	5071
1924–1925	702671–710164	7493			

MERMAIDS AND SIRENS

Certain objects are difficult to tame yet it is
their very strangeness that perpetuates my
curiosity and their appeal in my eyes ...
—Anon

Stories of mermaids and sirens have existed in various cultures for literally thousands of years; tales are abundant in Greek legend and elsewhere. Like all mythological entities, the stories that surround them have spawned a curious fascination with any associated artefacts. We know that mermaids don't actually exist, but strangely enough there seem to be quite a few of them in existence. Any 15th-century sailor would have firmly believed in these elusive sirens!

What is certain is that sailors frequently mistook creatures such as manatees and dugongs as mermaids. These belong to a genus known as the *Sirenia* order of aquatic mammals and it's easy to see how they could be mistaken for human-like creatures. However, the Japanese also have an extremely strong history of mermaid folklore; traditional representations in their art and literature often portray them as far more grotesque than our European idea of a beautiful half-human, half-fish. Known as *ningyo*, meaning 'human fish', they usually take the form of a cross between a fish and a monkey, which is quite interesting in that the earliest known specimens of mermaids to arrive in Europe were indeed made from half a monkey and half a fish cleverly stitched together, sometimes with other animal parts added, such as fur and bat wings.

There are various examples of such mermaids in Japanese shrines, some dating from the 15th and 16th centuries, and it seems that Japan may well have been the source of the best mermaid fakes. No early 'museum' or cabinet of curiosities would have been without such a specimen and such curious oddities can be identified in European 16th- and 17th-century engravings. For a nation surrounded by the ocean it is hardly surprising that such strong myths exist, and there are even documented stories of early European visitors to Japanese waters sighting these grotesque mermaids.

By the 18th and 19th centuries the Japanese public had gained quite a hunger for such 'side-show' freaks of nature and as a result these cleverly constructed and often ancient-looking specimens caught the attention of entrepreneurs in Europe and America. So convincing were some of these creatures that even the *American Journal of Science* mentions them in 1863:

> We should judge that the Japanese must have considerable knowledge of the lower animals to be able to produce factitious congeries, so nearly agreeing with nature and so well calculated as to deceive even practiced naturalists.

The fact was that mermaids were big business and a good mermaid could generate considerable sums for its owner. Perhaps one of the most famous is the Feejee mermaid (also known as the Fiji or Fejee mermaid) made famous by the showman P.T. Barnum. He leased it in 1842 from an associate named Moses Kimball for

$12.50 a week and it toured the United States, causing controversy and making a fortune from what was essentially an elaborate hoax. Barnum even brought the Feejee mermaid to London in 1859 but sadly it disappeared sometime in the 1880s, thought to have been lost in a fire.

Examples of such 'mermaids' rarely come up for sale, but when they do they're expensive.

DID ELGIN STEAL THE MARBLES?

Tell me what you collect and tell me how you collect and I will tell you who you are
—Jean Willy Mestach

It's an emotive subject and one that intermittently has the Greek nation demanding the return of the Parthenon marbles; the most famous proponent of the cause was Melina Mercouri, actress and minister for Greek culture, who waged an emotive campaign for the return of the 'looted' marbles housed in the British Museum. She died in 1994. However, the argument smoulders on: did Thomas Bruce, the 7th Earl of Elgin, steal the marbles? It has been a matter of heated debate for the last 200 years and an accusation that also challenges the integrity and validity of the world's museums and the honesty of their collections.

The British Museum was established in 1753, largely based on the collections of Sir Hans Sloane. As the expansion of the British Empire took place, it was to be filled with the many acquisitions from Britain's new overseas territories. As the 'enlightenment' gathered pace, collections were sold to the museum and approved as acquisitions by the trustees; they sought to deal with the legalities of objects they were offered or acquired. The already famous diplomat and antiquarian Lord William Hamilton had sold the Porcinari Collection of Greek, Etruscan and Roman vases to the British Museum in 1772, having purchased it quite legitimately from the Porcinari family in Naples.

In 1798 Elgin was appointed as Ambassador to Selim III, Sultan of the Ottoman Empire. Greece was under Ottoman rule and Athens had been under their control since 1460. Prior to his appointment, Elgin had approached the British government to gain support for a venture to document the Parthenon marbles; this was rejected and he joined the ranks of self-financing 'saviours' who felt that they were perhaps doing a valuable job in recording and trying to preserve endangered antiquities. What is certain is that the venture cost Elgin dearly. He spent some £70,000 of his own money financing a team of artists and labourers under the supervision of court painter Giovanni Lusieri to take casts and draw the monuments. However, the removal of material, not just from the Parthenon but from the surrounding temples and treasury, raises other issues. Elgin was granted a firman by the Sultan – a type of licence or permission. The legality of the firman has been the main bone of contention ever since, made even more problematic by the fact that the original no longer exists.

Elgin began the removal of artefacts in 1801; it's

obvious that he saw the firman as a permission to do so, strengthened by the attestation that the huge damage already done to the Parthenon in the past provided good reason. In 1687 the temple had been bombarded by the Venetians. It was being used as an arsenal and the resulting explosion felled the roof and fourteen columns, severely damaging much of the sculpture. Although not a totally sound argument, there are those who suggest that had Elgin not removed the marbles, even less would have been left for future generations.

Elgin eventually sold the collection to the British Museum in 1816 for £35,000. An exhaustive investigation into whether or not he had legitimately acquired them took place and it was decided that the acquisition was legal. The Turks ruled Greece and had done so for several hundred years, plus they were extremely grateful for the help of the British in keeping Napoleon at bay. Detractors, even at the time, accused Elgin of blatant vandalism; the removal of the material did cause serious damage to the monument.

Subsequently, the British Museum has been accused of seriously harming the marbles by over-cleaning in the 1930s and deterioration through air pollution in London. Counter-arguments emphasise how pollution and acid rain would have done even more damage in Greece but such arguments tend to fall on deaf ears! However, the historical details of the 'paperwork' still remain a matter of great controversy and coupled with various other arguments for their return to the purpose-built modern museum in Athens it seems that the result of Elgin's actions are unlikely to ever go away.

WHAT IS ART DECO?

Art Deco is a design style that at its best is superbly striking, bold and original. However, what is often seen is a cheap mass-produced pretence to that style; not everything that dates from the 1920s and 30s is Art Deco! This might sound a little harsh but it's something that is true of most artistic or design movements; it's rather like a Chanel outfit being loosely copied for Topshop – there is a big difference between *haute couture* and High Street.

It's interesting to look at how 'high design' has affected our everyday lives. Long before Art Deco (I'll come back to its origins) there were various other important design styles including Baroque, Neoclassical, Gothic Revival, the Aesthetic movement, Art Nouveau and Arts and Crafts; then there were the contemporary styles to Art Deco, such as Modernism and Bauhaus. These were superseded in the post-war period by Mid-Century Modern, Brutalism and Pop Art to name but a few. Many such movements evolved out of common ideals, such as the revival of craftsmanship or the exploitation of mass-production techniques, and most countries had their own versions of and names for these styles.

Most of us are familiar with the most famous of these movements, particularly Art Nouveau and Art Deco. Art Nouveau is characterised by its organic and sinuous lines; the French were undoubtedly the best exponents of the genre and the iconic designs of Hector Guimard for the entrances to the Paris Metro system epitomise the fluidity of this often extraordinary style. Other designers stepped seamlessly between different styles and René Lalique did so effortlessly, moving from his awe-inspiring jewellery creations of the Art Nouveau period to the wonderful and much sought-after glass designs of the Art Deco period. A rare *cire perdue* (lost wax) cast glass vase by Lalique recently sold for £280,000.

Art Nouveau lasted roughly from the late 19th century until about the end of the First World War. Art Deco arrived in the inter-war period, originating in the 1920s, and is largely seen as an antidote to the machine-age carnage of the First World War, symbolised by hedonistic flapper girls, skyscrapers and streamlined fast cars. The term 'Art Deco' is attributed to the French Modernist architect Le Corbusier, who used the phrase '1925 Expo; Arts Deco' in reference to the *Exposition Internationale des Arts Décoratifs et Industriels Modernes* (International Exposition of Modern Decorative and Industrial Arts), a world fair held in Paris, but it came into common usage in the 1960s.

The style of Art Deco is characterised by bold geometric designs, strong colours and lavish ornamentation but at the same time is often supremely stylish in its streamlined simplicity so emblematic of speed and industrial progress. The style infected every aspect of life from industrial and product design to architecture, fashion, film, decorative arts and entertainment. Exotic dancer Josephine Baker and her pet cheetah Chiquita symbolised both the style and excess of the Roaring Twenties.

Deco undoubtedly has its roots in Cubism, Modernism and Futurism and it's easy to see where the lines blur between various exponents of these styles. However, at its most pure – in examples such as the Chrysler Building in

New York, designed by William van Alen; the interiors of ocean liners such as the *Normandie*; and visual arts pieces such as the poster for the film *Metropolis* – Deco is a stunning style full of glamour and hope. What did the British contribute to the style? Well plenty, but there are certain people who would be most upset if I didn't mention Clarice Cliff. Sadly, Art Deco was also an overly optimistic interlude before the horrors of the Second World War.

THE QUEEN'S KNICKERS

It's amazing what people collect, and it certainly doesn't stop at objects of intimate apparel. I once paid a visit to the famous Frederick's of Hollywood Lingerie Museum where items belonging to Elizabeth Taylor and Marilyn Monroe were tastefully displayed in glass cases. Alas, the museum is no more but vintage lingerie has long been big business; of course, there are those who like a bit of old-fashioned glamour and current trends have put a strong demand on the ever-dwindling supplies of original material, if you'll excuse the pun. However, it seems that a little bit of fame or historical notoriety will boost the price of your smalls quite dramatically. Madonna's famous corset with cone-shaped cups, designed by Jean-Paul Gaultier, sold at Christie's in 2012 for £30,000. Another creation invented to support Marilyn Monroe's assets proved far better value in 2009 when what can only be described as 'space age' technology was sold for £3,200. Not a thing of beauty, the over-engineered bra certainly performed a function but was surpassed in beauty and price by one of her lacy numbers that sold at the Hollywood Legends sale in 2010 for $7,000. However, both of these were recently put in the shade by the bra from her *Some Like it Hot* dress, which sold at Julien's Auctions in Beverly Hills for $28,125.

One pair of briefs that failed to find a buyer were a rather grubby pair of Elvis' pants that came up for sale at Omega Auctions of Stockport in 2012. They were known to have been worn at a concert in 1977 under one of his famous jumpsuits but failed to meet the £7,000 reserve – not surprising really, given the state of them! A much more attractive ensemble was the red silk La Perla set worn by Kylie Minogue on her 2012 calendar, which realised £5,000 for charity.

On a statelier note, some years ago I filmed one of Queen Victoria's stockings on the *Antiques Roadshow*. It had apparently been rescued by a person in service and kept as a memento of the great lady. It was woven with a 'VR' cipher and I seem to remember valuing it at £100 or so. However, all records tumbled in 2008 when Hanson's auctioneers in Derbyshire auctioned a pair of Queen Victoria's stockings for a staggering £8,000. They were purchased by a museum. In the same sale a pair of her bloomers with a 50in waist made a pretty robust £5,000.

Not long afterwards, another pair of interesting knickers surfaced but this time there was a matter of decorum and taste to be considered. The silk monogrammed briefs, embroidered with an 'E' over a crown, were apparently left on an aircraft in 1968 by our present Queen on a state visit to Chile. They were part of the estate of the late Joseph de Bicske Dobronyi. He is described as an 'aristocrat, art collector, traveller and playboy' but no official confirmation as to the authenticity of the story or origin of the bloomers was forthcoming. They sold on eBay in 2012 (Jubilee year!) for £11,390 – perhaps the ultimate piece of royal memorabilia!

TREASURE TROVE – THE LAW

We all dream of finding treasure, but for some ardent metal detectorists this dream has become a reality. The metal-detecting fraternity and archaeologists have long had a love/hate relationship. Sadly, as in most cases, there are those among the hobbyists that have blackened the name of the responsible detectorists. The problem is, the rewards are potentially great, and as we've seen in recent years with some of the superb finds such as the Staffordshire Hoard, the Ringlemere cup and the staggeringly large hoard of 52,000 coins found near Frome in Somerset, the financial recompense can be huge. The temptation to flout laws of national statute seems obvious to the criminally inclined, but in reality there is little point as modern Treasure Trove law allows reported finds to be fully recompensed at their market value.

Prior to 1996, the law was literally medieval but a reworking of the Treasure law together with the inception of the government-funded Portable Antiquities Scheme (PAS) meant that people, particularly metal detectorists, were encouraged and made aware of the importance of reporting finds to a finds liaison officer (FLO) so that their context and any potential additional information that might be gleaned from their discovery was not lost forever. Sadly, the market is awash with stolen antiquities, many of which have no provenance or context, and this is highly detrimental to our understanding of our past. The success of the scheme has been enormous, with reported finds climbing tenfold.

The idea was not just to reel in valuable 'treasure trove' items but also to encourage the reporting of more mundane objects, those which often have useful information attached. Results early on in the scheme spoke for themselves. In the year 2000, 221 treasure trove items were reported; in 1995, one year before the laws were revised, it was just 24.

However, the success of the new scheme caused other problems. Britain's museums have limited acquisition budgets; unbelievably, the British Museum's budget is just a couple of hundred thousand pounds a year, which goes absolutely nowhere when you are trying to acquire a collection like the Staffordshire Hoard. (The finder and the landowner split £3.3 million between them – frankly a bargain in my opinion, given that there is no real precedent for this type of find being valued.) Consequently, the usual route to raise the funds is via the Art Fund (formerly the National Art Collections Fund), a charitable organisation which raises money by subscriptions and donations to save works of art for the nation. It raised £900,000 towards the Staffordshire Hoard so that the Birmingham Museum & Art Gallery and the Potteries Museum & Art Gallery, Stoke on Trent could keep the collection for the nation. The balance is then usually collected from benefactors and by public donation.

In the meantime the relationship between archaeologists and metal detectorists has moved on to a more mutually advantageous footing. When you look at the catalogue of major valuable archaeological finds in Britain over the last ten years, most of the discoveries have been made with metal detectors. The right attitude and standards have shown that both parties can work hand in hand to produce rewarding results.

There are however some anomalies in the Treasure Act and this was recently emphasised by the discovery of a Roman copper-alloy parade helmet near Crosby Garrett in Cumbria in May 2010. Now known as the Crosby Garrett helmet, it was sold at Christie's, London for £2.3 million in October 2010. It was not declared treasure trove as it is not made of precious metal. It seems legislation may be afoot to alter this deficiency in the law, as this is perhaps one of the most superlative objects of its type ever to surface. Guess who found it? A chap with a metal detector.

For the official summary definition of treasure, see the Portable Antiquities Scheme website: finds.org.uk

THE LIFE OF A MUDLARK

The foreshore of the river Thames in London is said to be one of the biggest archaeological sites in the world. For centuries the rubbish and detritus of this ever-evolving city was continually dumped into this great historical cesspit. The Thames was for centuries renowned as being like an open sewer; these days it's far different but the benefit of this foul soup was that it slowly produced an anaerobic mud (devoid of oxygen) that preserves entombed objects perfectly. This means that the foreshore is a veritable storehouse of amazing artefacts, spanning eons. The Society of Thames Mudlarks is an organisation that liaises closely with the Museum of London and operates under a special licence granted by the Port of London Authority. Membership is strictly limited and all significant finds are reported and logged by the museum. The Museum of London has many exhibits that were found on the Thames foreshore and these include all manner of objects ranging from medieval pewter pilgrim badges to Georgian jewellery – but most commonly occurring are the myriad pieces of clay pipe and medieval pins.

Despite the name 'mudlark' being associated with modern collectors of bits and bobs scavenged from the mud, the term has a much older meaning. In Henry Mayhew's work *London Labour and the London Poor* (1861–2) he interviews a young mudlark. Listed as 'Those That will Not Work' under the chapter heading 'Felonies on the River Thames', it seems that they were regarded as nothing more than common thieves, although they were doing nothing different to the many poor people all around the world who have scraped a living in this way.

Mudlarks were traditionally youngsters aged between eight and their late teens who scavenged a living on the river, salvaging anything of value. They were the poorest of the poor, raggedly dressed and often infested with vermin, scraping a few pence here and there by collecting lumps of coal that had fallen from the barges, old rope, pieces of canvas, fat, scrap iron and copper cast overboard from ships – all of this sold by weight. The price of iron would fluctuate but in 1860 it could be expected to sell for between ¼d and 3d. It was a hard life, ruled by the tides. The work was filthy with excrement; injury, infection and harassment by the police were perpetual hazards.

Of course, the myriad wharfs and docks that they plied have long since disappeared. It is interesting perhaps that many of the objects that absorb us today would have had no real value to a Victorian mudlark; now the hobby is regarded as a slightly eccentric and specialist pastime.

Mudlarks, from a 19th-century etching

ANIMAL, VEGETABLE OR MINERAL?

There is no debate! The killing of elephants for their tusks to satisfy a tourist's desire to buy a poorly carved

THE ANTIQUES MAGPIE

ivory souvenir is simply not acceptable. However, the whole issue of ivory and other animal- and botanical-related products in the world of art and antiques has become a complicated and sometimes contentious issue. We have to accept that historically we cannot alter the actions of our ancestors. Collecting butterflies or birds' eggs, the use of ivory, tortoiseshell, rhino horn and other 'by-products' from currently endangered species has been commonplace throughout history, both in art and for practical purposes. The historical list of extinctions is long and ever-increasing – dodos and the mighty moas and elephant birds of New Zealand and Madagascar were all either hunted into oblivion or affected by environmental issues. I've seen the African 'shooting diaries' of Victorian big-game hunters and they are quite staggering: hundreds of animals of all varieties shot for sport in just a few days.

From an auctioneer's point of view, it's been interesting to observe the barometer of acceptability (or distaste) that has risen and fallen over the decades. Anti-fur campaigns have come and gone, fashions change, but the legacy of our ancestral ways still surfaces in the form of fur coats, tiger-claw brooches and tortoiseshell tea caddies. So what is reasonable, what is acceptable in terms of collecting objects and artefacts manufactured and crafted by our ancestors from the parts of animals?

Well certainly in some circumstances there are strong moral issues. The argument that the continued trade in antique ivory objects encourages the trade in modern ivory, and therefore poaching, has always been highly debated. The value of rhino horn as a medicinal product on the

Asian markets has long catalysed the sale of unworked antique horns at auction, for use as a source; does this promote the terrible slaughter of rhinos? It is now illegal to sell unworked rhino horns at auction but just prior to the legislation being set in stone in 2012, there was a rush to sell antique horns. Auction houses were even broken into prior to sale, and at £40,000–60,000 per kilo, it's not difficult to see how criminals are incentivised by such potential gains.

The laws governing the sale of such products have become increasingly complex and are now governed by international conventions. Essentially, the main body that determines international trade and certification in animals, plants and their derivatives is CITES; DEFRA is responsible for the UK.

CITES has an enormous and sometimes seemingly impossible task to try to stop the continual wholesale slaughter and depletion of various species, but it ceaselessly endeavours to regulate or prohibit trade in certain species of plants, animals, corals and derivatives. These are all categorised within appendices I, II and III – Appendix I being the most controlled – to the text of the convention. For example, elephant ivory is in Appendix I, meaning that international trade is heavily restricted and in many instances banned completely.

DEFRA administers the British market and requires that any ivory that is imported or exported has to be made (meaning worked) prior to 1 June 1947 and have all the necessary certificates, i.e. a 'pre-convention exemption' certificate from CITES, even for 'antique' items. You must also be able to prove that it is antique. If a plain antique tusk is worked later it does not qualify and is immediately exempt from antique exemption status. Infringement can carry a seven-year jail sentence and unlimited fines. Tortoiseshell and rhino horn are also on the Appendix I list; even ivory piano keys can be subject to the rules!

The legislation also covers a diverse selection of plants. Lignum vitae, for example, is a slow-growing hardwood with interesting qualities. It was favoured for the production of candlesticks, mortars and medicinal containers in the 18th and 19th centuries. It's sometimes known as 'ironwood' and is even used in preference to metal bearings in some industrial applications. It's an Appendix II species. Also, be aware that it is illegal to sell any wild birds' eggs, irrespective of their age. Taxidermy is similarly governed by very strict rules and although there has been a renaissance in the use of natural history and taxidermy among collectors and decorators it is still subject to strong controls, particularly in areas such as birds of prey. The same also applies to butterflies.

Don't in all innocence think that because something is being sold, it must be legal to do so; but at the same time, it is permissible to look at things in their historical context and make a personal judgement about whether you want to own them – they are not all illegal!

NB – Every effort has been made to give an accurate view of current legislation in these matters but please note that this does not reflect the complete picture or constitute legal advice on buying or selling prohibited or protected animal or plant species. See www.cites.org and www.defra. gov.uk for more information.

PLASTIC FANTASTIC

plastic, *n.*

a synthetic material made from a wide range of organic polymers such as polyethylene, PVC, nylon, etc., that can be moulded into shape while soft, and then set into a rigid or slightly elastic form …

Origin: mid-17th century (in the sense 'characteristic of moulding'): from French *plastique* or Latin *plasticus*, from Greek *plastikos*, from *plassein* 'to mould'

—*Oxford English Dictionary*

Plastic is the material that we love to hate but seemingly can't do without. Its versatility knows few bounds and historically its development has led to amazing technological advancements and products that have provided collectors with a vast array of objects. From Barbie dolls to Bakelite light switches and Lucite handbags, where would we be without it?

The first plastics were not really plastics in the sense that we know them today. 'Natural' plastics such as horn and tortoiseshell were malleable materials that could be easily moulded using heat or compression. We generally associate the word with modern chemical-based products, but man-made materials have a much wider historic tale to tell. Semi-synthetics, which are chemically altered natural materials, were the next leap forward. When Charles Goodyear invented the process of vulcanising rubber in 1839 he made a valuable discovery. By heating the rubber with sulphur he found that it could be altered to produce a material of varying hardness, which he called **vulcanite**;

it was a popular medium in the Victorian period, used for everything from faux jet jewellery to false teeth.

Gutta-percha, similar to rubber, was also a brand name and a type of sap derived from the Palaquium gutta tree and was used from the early 1840s. Its chief application was for coating underwater telegraph cables but it was also used for the first commercial golf balls. Unfortunately, it becomes brittle when exposed to air so few items made of gutta-percha survive. The trees were also over-harvested in the 19th century, leading to a collapse in the supply. We know it these days as an inert infill for root canals.

Bois Durci is an interesting material based on a mixture of cellulose, finely ground wood 'flour' and strange ingredients such as albumen, blood or gelatine. It was patented in 1855 by François Charles Lepage. The dried powder was compressed under high pressure in steel moulds heated with steam and was used for a variety of applications ranging from commemorative portrait plaques to jewellery (larger items are sometimes marked 'Bois Durci').

Shellac was widely used for the manufacture of items such as gramophone records but could be mixed with all manner of fillers to produce objects such as the fancy 'union' frames for daguerreotypes and tintypes (types of 19th-century photograph – *see* Image Conscious, *page 74*). The term 'union' is often thought to be a reference to the American Civil War but actually refers to the union of shellac and the filler. Shellac is made from the excretions of a beetle found in India and Malaysia. The 'lac' was collected and made into a resin – interesting to imagine how anybody actually arrived at that!

Parkesine was patented in 1861 and displayed at the

International Exhibition of 1862 in Kensington, London, where it won a medal for product excellence. It was a very innovative material, imitating tortoiseshell and taking all manner of different colours that could be incorporated into the body of the plastic. In 1862 Alexander Parkes set up a company in Hackney Wick, London, but it went bankrupt within two years, possibly due to the fact that he endeavoured to keep the price down and could not meet quality production costs; objects didn't maintain their shape quite as well as expected! We now know this product as **celluloid** but it was Parkes that did most of the legwork prior to the American John Wesley Hyatt patenting the Celluloid brand name and product in the USA in 1869. Celluloid based on nitrocellulose was notoriously unstable and flammable; urban legends abound about exploding billiard balls made from the new product but these cannot be reliably substantiated.

Another English inventor, Daniel Spill, had been working in parallel with Hyatt and had patented a product called **Xylonite**. This was essentially celluloid. A number of costly court battles ensued but Parkes was eventually attributed as the inventor of celluloid. Improved methods of production eventually led to a stable product that became a mainstay of the plastics industry, with both Hyatt and Spill allowed to continue production under their own brand names.

Casein is another oddball plastic which began life in the early 20th century. Derived from cow's milk, casein is a protein that can be separated and soaked in formalin (formaldehyde solution) to produce a plastic that became popular for manufacturing buttons, fountain pen cases and knitting needles. Casein has to be machined rather than formed in moulds, so it was well suited to production from stock-based blanks – hence the large amount of buttons made of casein. It also takes colour well and can be polished using friction or a chemical dipping process.

The most famous of all 'plastics' and one that most of us know by its trade name is **Bakelite**. Patented in 1908 by Dr Leo Baekeland, a Belgian-born American chemist, Bakelite was the first thermosetting plastic, known as polyoxybenzylmethylenglycolanhydride. Dr Baekeland initially set out to find a substitute for shellac and in doing so built upon the research of earlier chemists into polymers. Bakelite was derived from a reaction between phenol and formaldehyde and it revolutionised many aspects of industrial and domestic design and manufacture. It was particularly useful for electrical and car components, with good insulating and heat-resistant properties. It proved versatile in the production of everything from radio cases to toys, jewellery, kitchen products, furniture and aircraft parts – in fact, it is still used in many applications today, despite all the more modern plastics that have since evolved. Baekeland christened it 'the material of 1,000 uses' and its versatility has made it a favourite among collectors. Iconic designs such as the Bakelite-cased circular Ecko AD-65 radio designed by Wells Coates in 1932 epitomise the Art Deco period and the use of this revolutionary plastic.

Distinguishing between some of these early plastics can be quite difficult. Other versions such as Plascon or Bandalasta, a thermosetting polymer, or Catalin, a cast phenolic variation on Bakelite that is valued for its vivid colours and variegated marbled finishes, came under the generic heading of Bakelite. Plastics such as Catalin are particularly valued by collectors of vintage radios who are prepared to pay thousands of pounds for some of the best examples. Such radios relied on the skill of the mixer to produce the unique finish of each cabinet, and this remains very much the appeal of many early plastics among today's collectors.

'Plastic' might seem like a throw-away word but it is far from it in collecting terms.

IMAGE CONSCIOUS

You don't take a photograph, you make it.
—Ansel Adams

We take it for granted: digital technology has made taking photographs easy; the idea of buying a film and working out that each image would cost 26 pence to develop, then leaving the film in a drawer for years, seems like a distant memory as we merrily snap away and download by the dozen.

In reality, digital technology is a relatively recent innovation. Invented in 1975 by Steven Sasson, an engineer at Eastman Kodak, it's ironic that a company that was so famous for major innovation and commercial success in the history of photography was eventually bankrupted by its failure to understand the significance of a major future technology – one that it had actually invented! It's clear that Kodak saw film as an unassailable medium for photography and as the whole basis of the company depended on it, it quietly swept the invention under the carpet.

If we place digital photography into the timeline of photographic history it quickly becomes apparent that photography is actually a very recent invention. The earliest commercial images of our ancestors date from the 1840s. Prior to that, you had to employ an artist to record a likeness.

One of the founding fathers of photography was a Frenchman called Louis Daguerre (1787–1851). His invention, the Daguerreotype, was announced in 1839 to the French Academy of Sciences and in exchange for a lifetime pension Daguerre allowed his rights to pass to the French government who then magnanimously allowed the process to be released 'free to the world'. However, by a strange twist of fate, this did not apply to Britain because Fox Talbot, a founding father of British photography, wrote to the Academy claiming that he had a prior claim to the invention without realising that the two processes were completely different. Daguerre's agent then filed a patent in the UK just days before the French government made it 'free to the world', meaning that a licence fee had to be paid in the UK to use the French process.

As you can imagine, the invention of photography was tantamount to landing a man on the moon and the collecting of photographic material, including images and equipment, is a vast field. However, it's also an area in which the historical record is continually moving as new discoveries are made about who made the first advances in photography. In recent years, the boundaries have moved considerably as the invention and attribution of the word 'photographer' has been ascribed to Thomas Wedgwood, son of the famous potter, Josiah Wedgwood. In reality it seems that processes involving the reproduction of images (or profiles of objects) on light-receptive silver nitrate-coated mediums such as glass and paper has existed since the 1790s, although they could not be reliably fixed to prevent them disappearing in strong light. Recent revelations suggest that a 'photogenic' image of a leaf attributed to Fox Talbot may indeed be by Wedgwood – this is a staggering development (no pun intended).

For collectors and museums alike, the pursuit of pioneering or unusual images is compelling. Early photographs of historic events or battles, ancient monuments, or famous individuals can command enormous sums. In 2011 a tintype of Billy the Kid, c.1880, sold in America for $2.3 million. In 2003 Christie's sold the first part of a collection of daguerreotypes from the hitherto relatively unknown French photographer Joseph-Philibert Girault de Prangey. He learnt the process of making daguerreotypes in 1841, possibly from Daguerre himself, and then set out on a three-year tour of North Africa and the Mediterranean. He produced more than 800 images and these are among the earliest known photographic images of many ancient sites such as the Acropolis; they were never exhibited in his lifetime and subsequently realised huge prices, many going to the collection of the Getty Museum in Los Angeles. One sold for over half a million pounds. When the stakes are this high, would you have any idea what a daguerreotype is?

It's an area that causes confusion, mainly because there are two other types of early photograph that look almost identical and are often mounted in similar frames. These are ambrotypes and tintypes. Whereas the daguerreotype is an image fixed on a silver-plated sheet of copper and mounted in a protective case, an ambrotype is fixed on glass using the wet plate collodion process. This resulted in a negative image which, when viewed on a black background, appeared positive. This was achieved by lacquering the back of the fixed image, sandwiching it in glass and then mounting it in a protective case. These were much cheaper to produce than daguerreotypes and became more popular by the late 1850s.

By the 1860s, these too had largely been supplanted by tintypes, sometimes known as ferrotypes. In fact, there is no tin in a tintype: the image is produced on a black lacquer background supported on a cheap iron-based plate using much the same method as an ambrotype. These were quicker and cheaper to produce than their forerunners, and far less fragile. Tintypes were a favourite medium of 'street' and 'beach' photographers, who could produce them quickly for their customers. For this reason, most of the images are portraits or family groups, often hand-tinted; they are widely available and relatively cheap. Usually the identity of the sitter is lost to history but examples with names and provenance, or taken by good photographers, will cost more.

COMIC BOOK HEROES

What would childhood be without comics? Like many facets of our youth, they are something that generate great nostalgia among adult collectors. I can remember with much fondness my father arriving home with the latest copy of the *Beano*, a comic that has become iconic for its characters such as Dennis the Menace, Gnasher and Minnie the Minx. I grew up on the *Dandy* and *Warlord*, graduating to *2000 AD* and the American DC Comics in my teens. This is an area of collecting with potentially high stakes. A copy of the *Beano* sold in 2004 for £12,100; it had a good provenance and was near mint, but putting values on comics can be difficult, particularly American comics where prices can literally run into the millions of dollars. Much of it comes down to condition, with a very strict grading system carried out by professionals such as the CGC (Certified Guaranty Company). The comics are graded, then 'slabbed' in tamper-proof plastic cases never to be opened again, together with a full list of defects or restorations and a grade code ranging from 0.5 (poor) to 10 (gem mint – a very rare grade). In effect, these comics primarily become investment commodities and you'll need deep pockets if you want to participate at the top of the market, most examples of which come from what are known as the Golden (late 1930s to late 1940s) and Silver (1956–1970) Ages of comics.

Here are the top ten most valuable comics in the world, based on the highest price realised on the highest known CGC grades (current speculative auction estimates, as rated by www.comicbooks.com, in brackets).

1. *Action Comics* No. 1, 1938. This comic has the first appearance of Superman. $1,500,000 ($1,750,000).
2. *Detective Comics* No. 29, 1939. This comic features the first appearance of Batman. $1,075,000 ($1,400,000).
3. *Amazing Fantasy* No. 15, 1962. Spiderman makes his first foray in this edition. $1,100,000 ($1,100,000).

4. *Superman* No. 1, 1939. Superman gets his own title for the first time. $250,000 ($600,000).
5. *Batman* No. 1, 1940. Batman gets his own title for the first time. $315,000 ($400,000).
6. *Flash Comics* No. 1, 1939. The debut appearances of Flash and Hawkman. $450,000 ($385,000).
7. *Marvel Comics* No. 1, 1939. The debut of the Human Torch and start of one of the biggest comic franchises. $367,000 ($375,000).
8. *Captain America Comics* No. 1, 1941. Captain America makes his first appearance. $343,057 ($350,000).
9. *Archie Comics* No. 1, 1942. The spoiler in the line-up with the Archie Andrews character beating some of the superheroes! $167,300 ($260,000).
10. *More Fun Comics* No. 52, 1940. Debut of the Spectre. $207,000 ($250,000).

I recently met a man who spent a good deal of his spare time hunting around car boot fairs for the free gifts that came attached to comics. He seemed to have several of them logged into his boot sale radar, including the scarce red plastic frisbee that came attached to the front cover of 'prog 1' (edition one) of the 1977 debut edition of *2000 AD* featuring Judge Dredd. A reasonable edition without the spinner could be worth around £50–100, he explained, whereas with a spinner the value would be more likely £150–200. Cost of spinner found separately – probably nothing. However, this seemed like quite a hard way to make a living. There's no accounting for the world of collectables.

MERCHANDISING MANIA

The earliest forms of tie-in merchandising were advertising gimmicks often given away free; early film- and animation-related merchandising based on Charlie Chaplin (c.1914), Felix the Cat (c.1919) and Mickey Mouse (c.1928) often took the form of articulated wooden, cloth, pinned card, plush or lead figures.

As the media became more sophisticated and audiences grew, so too did the opportunities for selling related material. Children wanted to emulate their film and comic book heroes, so the production of *Dan Dare* planet guns and *Star Wars* lightsabres evolved into an acceptable commercial ploy. Now each generation nostalgically looks back to the 'first-time around' memorabilia that symbolised their childhoods.

Companies such as Mettoy Playcraft Ltd of Swansea, famous for their Corgi brand of die-cast toys, quickly realised the power of tie-in products and wisely secured licences to some of the biggest films and television series of the 1960s and 70s, including James Bond, *Batman*, *The Saint*, *The Man from U.N.C.L.E.* and the Beatles film, *Yellow Submarine*. Many of their products are eminently collectable. Meccano Ltd, although less proactive than Mettoy, secured licences for the massively successful Gerry Anderson productions such as *Thunderbirds*, *Captain Scarlet* and *Joe 90*. These too can command high prices among collectors. From My Little Pony to *Doctor Who*, our collecting habits are continually moulded by the vast machinery of the merchandisers and it's a market that's worth billions of pounds.

THE DEATH AND BURIAL OF COCK ROBIN

Who killed Cock Robin? Well in this case, it was a man called Walter Potter (1835–1918). Potter was an eccentric self-taught English taxidermist who specialised in anthropomorphic tableaux back in the days when stuffing animals was an acceptable pastime for young boys. He was thought to have been inspired by the work of Hermann Ploucquet who displayed anthropomorphic work at the Great Exhibition of 1851.

In addition to carrying out conventional taxidermy, a popular form of decoration in the Victorian era, Potter began to assemble dioramas of animals in human guise performing human acts. His parents owned the White Lion pub in Bramber, Sussex, and Potter's hobby soon attracted visitors to the premises; such was the demand that in 1861 he opened a separate display in the summer house. Many people today would find the idea of stuffing kittens and baby rabbits abhorrent but in Potter's day the public were fascinated by his displays and he soon had to move to bigger premises in Bramber; the 'museum' became a major tourist attraction, so popular in fact that an extension had to be added to the local station platform.

Potter based several of his tableaux on well-known nursery rhymes, hence 'The Death and Burial of Cock Robin', a large diorama started at the age of nineteen, which included 98 birds, the parson represented by a rook and an owl as the grave digger. It took him seven years to complete. 'The Rabbits' Village School' (1888) featured 48 young rabbits variously sitting at desks or immersed in educational pursuits. 'The Kittens' Tea and Croquet Party' (c.1870) featured 37 kittens, apparently supplied by a local farm, and 'Athletic Toads' had eighteen common toads following various exercise regimes in a park.

Unfortunately, Potter suffered a stroke in 1914 and never recovered. On his death in 1918 the museum held over 10,000 specimens, but as sensibilities changed in the 20th century the enthusiasm for such things waned and the museum was increasingly forced to deflect claims of animal cruelty in the creation of its exhibits. The museum eventually closed in the 1970s and was first moved to Brighton and then on to Arundel, eventually being purchased by the owners of the famous Jamaica Inn in Cornwall where it continued to prove quite a popular attraction. Economic factors and the death of the resident taxidermist eventually led to the collection being offered for auction by Bonham's in 2003.

The national value of 'Potter's Museum of Curiosities' had already been raised; the 'Kittens' Wedding' tableaux had been featured in the Victoria & Albert 2003 exhibition 'The Victorian Vision'. An attempt to preserve the collection intact was mounted by Damien Hirst, who reportedly offered £1 million, but this was rejected by the auctioneers. The owners subsequently sued Bonham's over the decision but the sale went ahead and was attended by various celebrities eager to capture a piece of this unique menagerie. 'The Death and Burial of Cock Robin' realised £23,500 with the 'Kittens' Wedding' making £21,150. The sale total accrued over half a million pounds but was still far short of Damien Hirst's offer.

As our sensibilities have changed yet again, the historical context of the collection was realised too late; for all its macabre connotations, it's a case bemoaned by many.

DECODING ART

A picture is worth a thousand words
—Napoleon Bonaparte

Hidden messages and symbolism abound in art; in fact, there are so many that it would take a large tome to explain the myriad subjects and symbols that would allow you to totally decipher the contents of a major art gallery. It's a process that has evolved over thousands of years borrowing from antiquity and myth while often combined with an artist's predilection to perhaps state their political views or illustrate their scorn of society or certain people.

The fun in many ways is to know something of this form of artistic camouflage and the strong historical conventions that dictate the construction of pictures and sculpture throughout art history; knowing how to decipher the hidden aura of meaning that lies present, even in the simplest-looking artworks, can add layers of subtle meaning. Some are present in modern life and we are naturally acquainted with them; a laurel wreath for instance symbolises victory and comes from the ancient Greek and Roman traditions of presenting victors or achievers in both physical and cerebral pursuits with a laurel crown. Roman emperors used it to celebrate 'triumph' and modern Grand Prix winners are traditionally adorned with large laurel wreaths. Little wonder then that it was so popular with Napoleon; the possessor of a huge ego, he was much portrayed wearing a gilded laurel wreath.

We also know that a set of scales symbolises judgement or justice, a way of weighing good and evil, right and wrong, although the personification of meaning often complicates matters. Examples include the archangel Michael, who uses his scales to weigh souls; Mercury represented the same in antiquity. In Albrecht Dürer's great work 'The Apocalypse; The Four Horsemen', the human representation of famine can clearly be seen holding a set of scales. Cupid is another common theme in art, one that we take to symbolise love and desire; born of ancient mythology, his power is symbolised by the ubiquitous bow and arrow.

Taking a complicated picture and analysing the meaning within can be fascinating. I love the satirical nature of some 18th-century pictures; Hogarth is a favourite and it takes knowledge of history and politics to get to grips with all that Hogarth has to say. His comments can seem all too evident on an initial reading but 'Gin Lane' and 'Beer Street', two famous prints issued in 1751, go to great lengths to emphasise the less obvious subtext in the benefits of beer and the evils of gin. Gin was a major problem in 18th-century Britain, where the government's misplaced ideas on distilling and taxation had helped to create an industry that devastated sectors of society, causing massive rises in misery, destitution, infanticide, suicide and starvation. The despair of 'Gin Lane', set in the parish of St Giles, knows no bounds, with the inhabitants driven to all depths of depravity, prostitution and murder. The only beneficiaries of the scene are the distiller, Mr Kilman, the pawnbroker Mr Gripe and the undertaker. Hogarth's portrayal is shocking in its explicitness but full of important symbolism.

More subtle are the messages and symbols contained

'Gin Lane' by Hogarth

in religious art and portraiture. Colour can be an important factor. The Virgin Mary is often represented in blue because blue symbolises truth and clarity; it is the colour of the sky, which is nearer to Heaven. Black and white we all know as the colours of purity/good and death/evil. Animals are also important: an ape symbolises the base nature of man, meaning lust and avarice. Satan is sometimes portrayed as an ape and when depicted in chains this denotes sin conquered. Again, this is shown in Albrecht Dürer's 'Virgin and Child with Monkey', c.1498. A chained ape sits at the Virgin Mary's feet.

Social status, religion, profession, academic achieve-ment, religion and moral stance can all be represented by the inclusion of artefacts such as books, jewellery, clothes, animals and historical references. Symbols of mortality, such as skulls placed on tables, emphasise death as the great leveller. Family groups by artists such as Gains-borough and Zoffany were imbued with a new form of informality set in rolling landscapes and surrounded by the trappings of success and social standing. Sir William Hamilton (1730–1803), British Ambassador to the court of Naples, looks regal in his portrait by David Allan, a large Attic vase depicted in the background denoting him as a man of taste and a great collector of antiquities. A simple French portrait of an 18th-century aristocratic lady partially submerged in a sparkling pool and grasping a flowing urn becomes a symbol of fertility and abundance; a broken pitcher signifies a loss of innocence – such are the nuances that we often fail to read as we pass through a gallery.

SMASH IT UP!

The buoyant oriental markets have seen a massive rise in interest when it comes to buying and selling antiques. Prices have been stratospheric and ordinary Chinese citi-zens keen to advance themselves in life have been bringing out their family treasures and hidden heirlooms to see if they too are harbouring a fortune. The backlash against the destruction of China's heritage during the Cultural Revolution has been huge and many objects have been sold in China or smuggled out of the country to be sold at foreign auctions. Unfortunately, China does have a reputation for being the centre of the faking universe and the markets have been flooded with millions of fake ceramics and works of art which are being bought by inexperienced buyers. As a result the Chinese have come up with their own novel version of the *Antiques Roadshow* entitled *Collector's World*. The difference with the Chinese version is that after the experts have presided over the piece the audience gets to comment and vote as to whether the piece is genuine or not. The owner then decides whether to enter into a contract to abide by the decision of the experts, the outcome being that if it is pronounced fake it is smashed with a golden hammer. A bit more knife-edge than the BBC version!

> When is a clock not a clock? When it's a timepiece. The subtle difference here is that a clock or watch that doesn't strike or chime is known as a timepiece – a technical difference that might occasionally annoy the purists in the watch and clock fraternity.

WARHOL IN A SKIP

I'd asked around ten to fifteen people for suggestions. Finally one lady friend asked the right question, 'Well what do you like most?' That's how I started painting money
—Andy Warhol

We all love a good 'I found it in a skip' story and I've heard a myriad of tales on the *Antiques Roadshow* recounting how desirable objects have been rescued from bins, public tips and car boot sales. For those of you who are slightly sceptical about such tales there are plenty of well-documented instances of rags-to-riches finds. Working as an auctioneer was essentially the professionally sanctioned side of saving things from the skip. By using my accumulated knowledge to recognise which things were not rubbish I delighted in making sure objects were rescued from landfill.

The most surprising tales are when in all innocence people with no knowledge fatefully find and rescue things that turn out to be interesting or valuable artefacts. One such person was Darryl Kelly, a 56-year-old man from New York. In 2006 he was sanctioned to clear the studio apartment of a reclusive photographer called Harry Schunke. Sadly, Schunke had been dead for some days before being discovered; the studio was piled high with the detritus of a man who had been a photographer of the New Realist movement and worked with people such as Yves Klein, Christo and Claes Oldenburg. He had died without leaving a will and the public administrator was put in charge of the estate, which resulted in Schunke's archive eventually being sold at auction to the Roy Lichtenstein Foundation. This amounted to some 200,000 photographs and other material.

The residual contents of the apartment were cleared out by Kelly and a team of men, to be dumped. They filled six trucks but noticed that pieces were being taken by passers-by. He decided to keep some and stacked over

2,000 items in a cupboard without any real idea what they were. Sometime later Kelly was watching the *Antiques Roadshow* and it made him curious. He took advice and found that the collection included Warhol prints and maquettes by Christo. Part of the collection was sold at auction in 2013 for $226,224. The bulk was sold privately to the Lichtenstein Foundation for an undisclosed sum. Kelly said he would take his children to Disney World.

DROIT DE SUITE

Droit de suite is a somewhat controversial piece of legislation that gives artists and their heirs the right to receive a percentage of the sale price of the subsequent resale of any of their works, usually 1–5 per cent. It's a complicated issue and process that has now been implemented Europe-wide, although some differences exist in the nature of the art to which royalties are applied in different European countries.

The phrase *droit de suite* simply means 'the right to follow'. The right, or *droit*, applies to pictures, photographs and other works of art that are still in copyright, so it does not affect Old Masters, for example. Different rules apply outside of Europe but other countries do have similar schemes or legislation to protect artists' rights.

Droit de suite was originally set up by the French in the late 19th century to protect the families of poor artists whose pictures were later sold on for larger amounts, and this was felt to be particularly important for the families of artists killed in the First World War.

The arguments against the idea state that it is a restrictive practice that stifles the European art market in favour of other outside markets, or, alternatively, that it should apply not just to artists but to those who make equally fine works, such as furniture; after all, how do we define art? Additional problems seem to stem from the administration; large amounts of money are sitting on deposit because so many artists and their heirs are untraceable. Many dealers see it as an additional tax. They pay it on a picture purchased at auction and then it has to be paid again when it is sold. However, the 'tax' does not apply when pictures are traded privately.

Specialists say that implementation of droit de suite is necessary to halt the tide of forgeries and misattributions by forcing auction houses to be more careful about provenance. However, it remains to be seen whether the Eastern economies, where many fakes herald from, have the will to enforce similar schemes. In the meantime, the debate goes on in Europe.

THE FIRST MUSEUMS

Art, in itself, is an attempt to bring order out of chaos
—Stephen Sondheim

We know that people have collected curiosities and works of art for thousands of years, but in modern terms the definition of a museum is a collection specifically assembled for public appreciation. Undoubtedly, the first museums started off as private collections; these were mainly the preserve of the wealthy and included libraries and collections in ancient Greece, Rome and Egypt.

During the Renaissance it became fashionable to build 'museums' commonly known as 'Cabinets of Curiosities' or *Wunderkammers* (wonder rooms). Royalty, aristocrats and eccentrics vied for rare and unusual objects from the natural, supernatural and earthly worlds to make their cabinets more wonderful than the next.

Rudolf II, Holy Roman Emperor (1552–1612) was one such collector. His 'cabinet' was not just a collection for the sake of collecting; it was a statement of wealth, power and enlightenment, which gave rise to a myriad of questions, ones which rocked the very foundations of religious belief and the origins of life, the world and the known universe – the earliest collections were in fact the antithesis to Christian doctrine, full of mysterious unexplained and hitherto unknown specimens: what were fossils? Does the unicorn exist? It's not surprising, under these circumstances, that many great collectors also dabbled in the 'black arts' and alchemy; and Rudolf's pre-occupation with the 'occult sciences' such as astrology and alchemy put him among a growing band of people who effectively heralded the start of the scientific revolution.

Rudolf was a great patron of the arts and his *Wunderkammer* became a black hole sucking in everything of interest and value from far and wide. Accounts of John Dee's (also known as Dr Dee, consultant to Elizabeth I) audience with Rudolf suggest it didn't go well but as a fellow occultist, the collection would have been a must for Dee to experience. Apparently, he was kept waiting for weeks. Dee's own Aztec obsidian 'scrying' mirror can be found in the Enlightenment room at the British Museum.

TRADESCANT'S ARK

The honour of the oldest museum in Britain generally goes to Tradescant's Ark. Born in Suffolk in the 1570s, John Tradescant the elder's first major appointment was as head gardener to Robert Cecil, 1st Earl of Salisbury, at Hatfield House. It was under his patronage and subsequently that of George Villiers, 1st Duke of Buckingham, and eventually the King, as keeper of vines and silkworms, that he gained his reputation as a well-travelled naturalist and collector. The *Musaeum Tradescantianum*, also known as Tradescant's Ark, was an assemblage of natural and man-made objects collected by John and his son.

The museum was situated in Vauxhall, south London on the modern site of Tradescant Road; the earliest accounts date from 1634 and existing contemporary literature from travellers and Tradescant himself gives us a wonderful insight into the nature of the collection. Access could be gained by payment, although this did not sit well with the educated classes; riff-raff were not deemed worthy of such things! Tradescant obviously used his connections and patronage to pursue 'Anything that is strang [*sic*]' and one letter to a seafaring merchant reads like a shopping list of the weird and wonderful: 'River horses head of the Biggest kind ... sucking fishes ...

habits weapons Instruments … all sorts of serpents etc., etc.' Georg Christoph Stirn, a visitor from Nuremberg in 1638, describes some of the things that he saw: 'The hand of a mermaid, the hand of a mummy … a small piece of wood from the cross of Christ … a toad fish … an instrument used by the Jews in circumcision … the robe of the King of Virginia.' Tradescant's museum became famous; no worthy visiting London would have missed it off the itinerary.

After his father's death in 1638, John Tradescant the younger took over his father's mantle, continuing his work for both the King and the Ark. One Elias Ashmole, collector and lawyer, befriended John through donating

John Tradescant the elder (left) and younger (right)

objects for the museum and financing the publication of the *Musaeum Tradescantianum* catalogue. To Tradescant Ashmole mooted concerns about the future preservation of the museum. The death of John's son in 1652 undoubtedly highlighted the uncertain future faced by the institution; John signed a document passing the collection to Ashmole for just a shilling. Hester, John's wife, realised that they had effectively been tricked and when John died in 1662 she resisted Ashmole's claims to the collection. Unfortunately he had risen in stature by then and the case came in front of the Lord Chancellor, whom Ashmole knew. The judgement went against Hester and Ashmole took the whole collection. She was later found drowned in her pond.

He did eventually donate the collection to Oxford University, which is why the collection is now called the Ashmolean Museum. It opened in 1683 and is regarded by some as the first true purpose-built public museum in Britain. Ironically Hester had determined to do exactly the same thing. Various exhibits still survive from Tradescant's original collection, notably 'Powhatan's mantle', or the 'King of Virginia's cape', as it is known. Powhatan was the father of Princess Pocohontas and the deerskin cape or hanging is recorded as having been at the Ark in 1638.

> The earliest museums on the Continent include the Capitoline Museum in Rome, which dates back to 1471 when Pope Sixtus IV donated a collection of important Roman statuary.

METAL GURU

People seem to get into a constant muddle with their metals and it's a particularly messy area, rife with mis-description, in the world of antiques. Alloys are the biggest problem. They've been around for almost as long as metals have been worked; the ancients used naturally occurring alloys such as electrum: a mixture of gold, silver and trace metals. It was particularly favoured for coinage by the Lydians and Greeks. Granted, some alloys can be quite difficult to tell apart, especially when more common ones are patinated to look like other, more valuable, ones. However, there are a few pointers that you can consider when assessing a potential purchase.

Bronze is commonly confused with **brass**. Bronze is a mix of mainly copper and tin, as opposed to brass, which is primarily copper mixed with zinc. The colours do differ but this also depends on the ratio of the constituents. Brass tends to have a dull yellow colour and is usually left 'raw'; bronze tends to be a reddish-orange colour with a man-made, chemically induced finish that can range from almost black to almost red. Bronze often has other elements added, such as phosphorus (phosphor bronze), which is useful for marine applications, but in the world of antiques it is more likely to be formed into sculptural works. Brass suits domestic applications better, so you are far more likely to find items such as doorknobs and letter-boxes cast from it.

Bronze has been around some 5,500 years and was used by civilisations the world over for everything from weaponry to decorative sculpture – hence the expression

'Bronze Age'. **Bell metal** is a form of bronze with a much higher copper content. As the name suggests, it is used for casting bells but was also used for cannon, particularly in the East, and for cooking utensils and mortars.

Due to bronze being expensive, manufacturers in the 19th century wanting to supply an up-and-coming middle class with affordable decorative items needed a cheaper substitute. They used an alloy commonly known as **spelter**, which is a mixture of zinc and lead. This was used extensively on the Continent and especially by the French; we see huge amounts of late 19th- and early 20th-century figures, clock cases, Art Nouveau and Art Deco sculpture produced in this way. Spelter could be painted to simulate bronze but has none of its qualities. It gets brittle and crystalline with age and can often be seen with cracks and finely bubbling paint caused by oxidisation.

Pewter has been in use for several thousand years and was utilised by the Egyptians and Romans; we tend to associate this alloy with household implements dating from the medieval period right through to the 19th century. Traditionally made from tin with small amounts of copper, antimony and bismuth, it's a soft alloy with a low melting point often used for tankards, spoons and chargers but also favoured in the Art Nouveau and Arts and Crafts period. It acquires a very deep grey colour with age but will shine to a silver-like finish if professionally polished.

Other less common alloys can command greater interest among collectors. Sometimes seen in auction catalogues is the alloy **paktong**. This was invented by the Chinese and is a mixture of zinc, copper and nickel. It closely resembles silver, tarnishes very slowly and was imported into Europe in the 18th century and used by craftsmen to cast objects such as candlesticks. Paktong objects are highly prized and realise just as much as, if not more than, their silver equivalents.

Here are a few other alloys that pop up in the world of art and antiques:

Pinchbeck – copper and zinc
Billon – copper and silver
Gunmetal – copper, tin and zinc
Corinthian bronze – copper, gold and silver
Nickel silver – copper and nickel
Rhodite – gold and rhodium
White gold – gold, nickel and palladium
German silver – nickel, copper and zinc
Britannia silver – silver and copper
Britannia metal – tin, antimony and copper

Troy ounces are a vestige of the Roman system of weights and measures, one that has endured for millennia and is still used for the weighing of precious metals today. The name comes from the town of Troyes in France, and one Troy ounce equals 31.103 grams or 1.097 avoirdupois ounces (the measure still commonly used in many English-speaking countries, based on sixteen ounces to the pound; *avoirdupois* comes from the Anglo-Norman French).

THE GOLD STANDARD

Carat or karat? These two words lead to some confusion, chiefly due to some countries, namely America, using the word karat to define gold purity and carat to define the weight for gemstones, whereas in the UK we tend to use the word carat universally with karat being used as an 'alternative'. It is often abbreviated to 'ct'. However, you do sometimes see items in the UK described as '14K' simply because they will be stamped with that standard mark, which is a universally acceptable way of defining the gold purity as 58.5 per cent. Twenty-four carat is pure gold, but it is generally mixed with 'fillers' due to its softness. These are usually copper, silver, palladium, platinum and nickel.

Here is a table of gold purities with the carat number. Those entries in bold are the carat numbers commonly marked on jewellery. The bracketed numbers denote stamps commonly used to signify that purity.

	Gold content (purity)
24 carat	**99+%**
22 carat (917)	**91.6%**
21 carat	87.5%
20 carat	83.3%
18 carat (750)	**75.0%**
15 carat	62.5%
14 carat (583)	**58.5%**
10 carat (417)	41.7%
9 carat (385)	**37.5%**
8 carat	33.3%
1 carat	4.2%

Gold prices have been fluctuating wildly in recent years. This has led to a rash of high street and postal gold scrapping services – beware, these exist to make money and pay less than the actual value of the gold.

> Where the term carat is applied to gemstones (and pearls), this follows an agreement on the definition of the metric carat adopted in 1907 at the Fourth General Conference on Weights and Measures; it was later accepted internationally, meaning that one carat is equal to a fifth of a gram (0.2g).

TAVERNIER'S LAW

Jean-Baptiste Tavernier (1605–1689) was a famous French diamond merchant whose travels in the Orient in the 17th century – some 180,000 miles through Persia and India – are documented in *Les Six Voyages de Jean-Baptiste Tavernier* (1676). In 1638 he embarked upon a major expedition which took him to the court of the Great Mogul Emperor Shah Jahan and the kingdom of Golconda. At this point in history, India was the only known source of diamonds and Tavernier's visit to the mines was unprecedented. The region, in the modern state of Andhra Pradesh, had a legendary status for the large and valuable gems that emanated from there; the Indians had fostered mythical scenarios of large venomous snakes that protected the stones, which could only be recovered by eagles. This was to be the precursor to Tavernier's future in the diamond trade.

One of his most famous acquisitions was the Hope Diamond, a fabulous blue gem variously known as *Le Bijou de Roi* ('the king's jewel') and the Tavernier Blue. The stone has an incredible history. It was sold to Louis XIV as part of a 'package' of 990 diamonds from Tavernier's travels. It went missing during the French Revolution and resurfaced many years later but in a different cut; it has since been proven from 18th-century sketches of the stone and the recent discovery of a hitherto unknown lead model in the *Muséum national d'Histoire naturelle* in Paris conclusively to be the main part of the Tavernier Blue. It weighs 45.52 carats and now resides in the Smithsonian Natural History Museum in Washington DC. It is believed to be insured for $250 million.

The equation below is known as 'Tavernier's Law' or the 'Indian Law' and it's a basic calculation to show how gem stones increase in value due to their carat size. You don't just double the value of a diamond if it's twice as big! Larger stones are rarer and go up in price in greater leaps and bounds. Of course, there are exceptions because large, badly flawed rubies, for example, are very common and can't easily be cut; consequently they have a low value. By modern standards this formula is really a bit of fun because colour (particularly with fancy diamonds), clarity and the density of different stones comes into play.

The equation is:

$$Wt^2 \times C = \text{Price}$$

i.e. Take the weight (*Wt*) of the diamond you want to value, square it and multiply by a base price (*C*) derived from a similar stone – not very scientific but interesting nevertheless!

Here's how the price of a diamond might increase with this formula applied to a £1,000-per-carat base price.

1ct	£1,000
2ct	£4,000
3ct	£9,000
4ct	£16,000
5ct	£25,000
10ct	£100,000

> In the world of diamonds, a paragon is a flawless stone of at least 100 carat (20g).

DEAD AND GONE

It seems somewhat macabre but the photographing of deceased family members was common practice in the 19th and early 20th centuries, particularly with young children. This has given rise to a very popular field of collecting known as post-mortem photography. Child mortality rates were high then and a photograph was a way of commemorating and immortalising a loved one; for many families, it might be the only image of the child and the only photograph of the family together.

Interestingly enough, if you have ever looked at Victorian photographs, even ones of your own forebears, you may well have looked at an image of a dead person without even realising it. Some are obvious, particularly with infants: babies are often posed in cribs or on cushions with favourite toys and flowers. Some are far more difficult to divine because they may depict a mother and father holding an infant that just looks fast asleep. Bibles are often included in compositions. It's also not uncommon for brothers and sisters to pose with dead siblings, perhaps with their arm around them, or for whole families to surround a dead child or relative, in effect camouflaging the true nature of the picture (particularly when they are all smiling).

Tell-tale clues in the composition can be the metal frames used to support the corpses, particularly with adults. These are often regarded as methods of keeping people still for long exposures, but it's not always the case. Sometimes it's just possible to see part of the stand protruding from behind a foot; otherwise you would have no idea that the person was deceased at all. Other indicators might be strategically placed props such as the odd book supporting a body; these are the clues you need to get you sleuthing – not everybody's cup of tea, but don't forget: higher mortality rates meant that attitudes to death were different.

IN THE FACE OF DEATH

Death masks were once a popular funerary rite and a way of preserving the features of royalty and prominent persons post-mortem. Napoleon was no exception: a cast of his face was taken two days after his death on St Helena on 7 May 1821. It was made by the surgeon Francis Burton, of the 66th Regiment of Foot, apparently much to the consternation of the Frenchmen who had attended Napoleon – God forbid an Englishman be allowed to do it! Also, so history relates, the delay in taking the mask was due to a shortage of plaster and fractious exchanges about who should be allowed to take the cast. It is thought that Napoleon's features altered significantly in these two days. A mask known as the 'Boys cast' after the Reverend Richard Boys, the senior chaplain of St Helena, one of only two original examples remaining in private hands, was sold on 19 June 2013 by Bonham's auctioneers, on behalf of a member of the Boys family, for a hefty £169,250.

BULLET POINT

A collection to which nothing can be added and from which nothing can be removed is, in fact, dead!
—Sigmund Freud

Think of something rather morbid and I can guarantee you that there will be someone out there prepared to collect it; but had you ever considered items related to assassination attempts? I first became interested in the history of such items many years ago after a visit to Konopiště Castle in the Czech Republic. There in the castle museum was a case containing 'the bullet that started World War I'. Fired by assassin Gavrilo Princip, the bullet that ended the life of Archduke Franz Ferdinand, heir to the Austro-Hungarian throne (his wife Sophie was also murdered) has taken on an almost legendary status as a controversial catalyst for the future slaughter in the trenches.

Further investigation of the subject led me to the first documented British assassination of a head of state with a firearm: James Stewart, 1st Earl of Moray, and Regent of Scotland. He was shot by James Hamilton of Bothwellhaugh in 1570, an ardent supporter of Mary Queen of Scots. It's a complicated political intrigue; Scotland was racked with divisive infighting and religious division. Stewart was mortally injured and died some hours later. The gun, known as the Bothwellhaugh carbine, still exists.

Ever heard of Spencer Perceval? Not many people have, but he has the grim epitaph of being the only British prime minister to be assassinated. He was shot in the lobby of the House of Commons on 11 May 1812 by a man called John Bellingham. Bellingham was a disgruntled bankrupt who had been imprisoned in Russia; he felt that the British government had done too little to help secure his release. He was hung for the crime despite his counsel pleading insanity.

I have been unable to track down the bullet that killed Perceval, but it wasn't so difficult to find the piece of lead that marked the demise of one of Britain's greatest heroes – Nelson. The bullet that killed him is displayed in the Grand Vestibule of Windsor Castle.

No one could really hazard an accurate estimate for the value of such an item, but a rather interesting artefact of similar historic importance was recently offered for sale by the London Fabergé specialists Wartski. A piece of lead shot that narrowly missed the Czar in 1905 during a regimental gun salute for the Great Blessing of the Waters on the frozen river Neva in St Petersburg is mooted as a catalyst for the 1905 revolution. One of the guns was loaded with 'live' shot and although a commission concluded that it was an accident, it was regarded by many as an attempt on the Czar's life. As the shot ricocheted around, one piece rolled at the Czar's feet and the young Grand Duke Nicholas Nicholaievitch picked it up, later having it mounted by Fabergé and presenting it to the Czar as a souvenir of the event. Although it didn't harm Nicholas, it's seen as an important factor in the eventual demise of the Russian royal family. Price: £500,000.

Unbeknown to many are the several attempts that were made on the life of Queen Victoria – seven, in fact. Some involved firearms charged with just the powder and were no more than the protestations of madmen – although I'm sure the Queen didn't see it like that. President Lincoln was not so lucky: the first US president to be assassinated, the bullet that killed him was fired by John Wilkes Booth on 14 April 1865, and can be found at the National Museum of Health & Medicine, Silver Spring, Maryland.

Those of you now wondering 'What about the bullet that killed John F. Kennedy?' should consider – notwithstanding that that particular projectile was fragmentary – that the collecting of artefacts that raise such moral issues seems to be determined very much by the amount of time that has elapsed. As first-hand accounts and memories fade with the passing of successive generations, it becomes more acceptable to collect such oddities. The rifle that killed Kennedy became the subject of much court action at the time, as rights to its ownership were traded by Oswald's widow Marina to the Denver oilman and gun collector John J. King. He sued the American government for $5 million for withholding it but it was later ruled that he had no right of ownership to either the rifle or the pistol that Lee Harvey Oswald had owned. They are both now kept in secure location at the National Archives and Records Administration Building in College Park, Maryland – value: unknown.

KEY MAN

Collecting keys is a popular hobby known as cagophily. Cagophilists have an infinite variety of material available and some tend to specialise in certain areas, such as steam ship keys, patent lock keys, etc. It's an area that's far more absorbing than you might imagine, with ancient, medieval and even modern keys encompassing superb craftsmanship, beauty and history in their creation. There are also keys that capture the imagination; one such example was a key from the crow's nest on the *Titanic*, which was sold in 2007 for £90,000 by auctioneers Henry Aldridge & Son. This small key with attached tag was for the binocular cabinet. By a strange twist of fate it was left in an officer's pocket who was transferred off the ship just before it sailed. He forgot to hand it to his fellow officer. This raises the question of whether or not the iceberg would have been spotted had they been able to open the binocular box.

DO GIRLS LIKE PLAYING WITH TRAINS?

Toy trains have traditionally been a male preserve, but one famous American toy company tried to challenge this convention. Lionel had been producing toys since 1901 but were best known for their trains. Renowned for their large-gauge locomotives and rolling stock, they eventually fell into line with the standard 'O' gauge used by their competitors and European manufacturers.

Lionel almost went out of business during the Depression; toy trains were a luxury and sales were poor. The company was saved by a cheaply produced Mickey and Minnie Mouse wind-up handcar which sold for $1 (very popular with modern collectors), and fortunes were revived. However, by the 1950s, trade was lagging again, mainly due to the new types of exciting toys that were available – space toys in particular. Lionel hit back in 1957 with a train set aimed at the female market, pepping up one of their standard ranges but in bright pastel colours such as pink, lilac and yellow. Guess what? It was a dismal failure.

As is so often the case with such commercial failures, they became scarce through lack of sales and are now worth as much as £5,000 a set in mint-boxed condition.

So, unfortunately for Lionel, the answer to the initial question is one that they should have seen coming: no, girls don't generally like playing with trains.

BALLS

The first golf balls were made of boiled goose feathers stuffed into a stitched leather 'ball'. When they dried, the feathers expanded and formed a rock-hard sphere known to collectors as a 'feathery'. They are very rare and do not generally survive in pristine condition. A good example could cost as much as £10,000.

By around 1850, the feathery had been superseded by the gutta-percha ball, known as a 'gutty'. Initially smooth, they were also textured by hand and later made in two-part metal moulds. A smooth gutta-percha is a rare thing and could cost £4,000–5,000.

With the advent of the rubber-cored ball, appearing c.1900, the basis for modern golf balls was established. Initially made in different sizes and weights with names such as the 'Jellicore', the 'Colonel' and the 'Ace', golf balls were standardised in Britain in 1921, the resultant ball being known as the 1.62 (a reference to its diameter in inches). Americans remained different with a 1.68 until all was unified in the 1980s with the American size. Early rubber-cored dimple balls can cost as little as £100 in good condition but rare designs such as the J.P. Cochrane 'map of the world' ball from c.1908 could cost you £3,000–5,000.

If you are unfamiliar with your golf requisites then you need to brush up on your collectable clubs because golf can mean big money among serious collectors. So if you don't know the difference between a cleek, a mashie, a lofting iron, a niblick and a brassie then you're scuppered before you even begin. The most valuable antique club ever sold is an 18th-century long-nosed putter attributed to the maker Andrew Dickson of Fife, sold by Sotheby's New York in 2007 for $181,000.

À LA FRANÇAISE OR À LA RUSSE?

Have you ever wondered why the family crests on French antique flatware (cutlery) are on the back, unlike British flatware where they are engraved on the front? Well, the answer is quite simple. We set our tables in a traditional style borrowed from the etiquette of Russian formal banqueting whereby we place the tines of our forks facing upwards rather than downwards as is the French habit – hence the necessity for the French to put their crests on the back of the flatware.

The French did in fact utilise *service à la Russe* in the early 19th century and it caught on later in Britain. The French tradition of putting all the food on the table at once was superseded on formal occasions by *service à la Russe*, which meant the courses would appear as and when required. It's the method we tend to favour today, although it's fun to occasionally set the table in the French style and make your guests eat their cheese before their pudding.

HARD-PASTE OR SOFT-PASTE?

If there was ever an industrial secret worth stealing it was the age-old Chinese recipe for making hard-paste porcelain.

Although the origins of porcelain are thought to be over 2,000 years old, the invention of Chinese 'white gold' translucent porcelain happened sometime in the 9th century. Its enigmatic and secret qualities remained the goal of European ceramicists for centuries until the alchemist Johann Friedrich **Böttger** was forcibly teamed with another inventor and alchemist, Ehrenfried Walther von Tschirnhaus. While pursuing the method for turning base metal into gold, the unwilling detainee was ordered by King Augustus II of Poland to crack the recipe for porcelain, which was achieved in 1707. The discovery remained secret until the process was perfected, leading to the founding of the Meissen factory; von Tschirnhaus, who was undoubtedly highly instrumental in the discovery, unfortunately died before the factory became well established, which left Böttger historically to take most of the credit.

Research in recent years has credited von Tschirnhaus' importance but prior to the invention of hard-paste porcelain in Europe the Chinese had essentially monopolised a product that was the envy of Western ceramic manufacturers. Hard-paste porcelain was originally a mixture of kaolin and processed micaceous and feldspathic rock known as petuntse, fired at a very high temperature, around 1,400°C.

Soft-paste porcelains made in Europe from the 15th century onwards in imitation of Chinese porcelain were often formulated from clays and powdered glass known as frit; later, ingredients such as feldspars and calcium phosphate were also used. Soft paste is fired at lower temperatures (1,100–1,200°C) and unlike hard paste is less malleable when worked, and is more prone to deformation in the kiln.

It can take a little practice to tell the difference but hard-paste porcelain has a more glass-like appearance; soft-paste is more granular and gritty.

'Clobbering' is a 19th-century slang expression for over-painting or enamelling ceramics, particularly Chinese blue and white porcelain. The colours were either cold-painted or re-fired and the technique was popular for pepping up ceramics and rendering them more attractive for the European market. In hindsight, some clobbered wares have been massively devalued by the process; lowlier artefacts such as ginger jars might be enhanced from a decorative or historical point of view.

In modern jargon clobbering means to overwrite computer files.

WILLOW PATTERN

There's a great deal of myth surrounding the origins of the famous willow pattern so popular on British ceramics. Contrary to perceived wisdom, it was invented by the English in response to the popularity of Chinese ceramics in the 18th century. The credit for the design is given to Thomas Minton and dates from c.1790.

A myth also grew up about the allegory within the decoration, which apparently tells the story of two lovers, the daughter of a wealthy Mandarin and a young man of lower caste. Already promised to a duke, the daughter and her lover make their escape to an island where some years later the duke catches up with them and has them put to death. It's a good marketing ploy!

The pattern comes in many colours and variations and

was a staple of the Staffordshire factories, particularly in the 19th century.

The willow pattern

CRASH MAIL

Collecting stamps is a far more complicated business than you might imagine. Philatelists are not just restricted to licking hinges and mounting their treasures in albums, there are several other specialist areas within the hobby; one in particular is the collecting of 'crash covers'. In philatelic terms this means mail retrieved from air crashes, shipwrecks, train crashes and other accidents. The mail is generally marked as recovered or damaged before being sent on. It may sound morbid but it's a popular facet of collecting, particularly early air-related accidents; imbued with a sense of tragedy and history, they provide a tangible reference to events such as the crash of the Hindenburg airship at Lakehurst, New Jersey on 6 May 1937. Some 367 items out of 17,609 pieces of mail survived that disaster and now sell for an average of £10,000–30,000 each.

THE VALUE OF COURAGE

The Victoria Cross is the highest military decoration that can be awarded to members of the armed forces of Britain, Commonwealth countries and previous territories of the British Empire. The medal was introduced by Queen Victoria on 29 January 1854 to honour valour in the Crimean War and was traditionally thought to be cast from the bronze of cannon captured at Sebastopol, although scientific analysis has shown that it is more likely to have come from Chinese cannon captured by the Russians. The remaining piece of bronze cascabel (the large knob at the end of a cannon) kept for this purpose weighs just 10kg, enough for a further 87 medals to be cast. It is kept in a secure vault.

There have been 1,351 Victoria Crosses awarded and only three double recipients. Just fourteen have been issued since the Second World War. Its importance as a mark of 'most conspicuous bravery, or some daring or pre-eminent act of valour or self-sacrifice, or extreme devotion to duty in the presence of the enemy', and its rarity, have made it legendary.

The value of the medal in financial terms has risen dramatically in recent years. The last remaining Australian Gallipoli VC, awarded to Captain Alfred Shout, was sold in 2006 for £406,716. The double VC of Captain Noel Godfrey Chavasse was acquired privately by the Michael Ashcroft Trust in 2009 for a reported £1.5 million. Lord Ashcroft's collection of VCs constitutes over one-tenth of the medals awarded and is now on display at the Imperial War Museum in London after he generously donated the collection and £5 million for the museum to build a new gallery. Lord Ashcroft's philanthropic motives do justice to a subject that is actually valueless in real terms.

The colour purple has been used since ancient times primarily to denote status; hence the imperial use of purple in ancient Rome. One reason for its elite and symbolic importance was its huge expense. The dye used for 'Tyrian purple' or 'royal purple' comes from certain species of predatory sea snails and whelks, although some species produce less vibrant shades – the spiky-shelled murex snails are the most valued. Several thousand snails will produce less than a gram of dye. Antique fabrics dyed in purple are likely to be of royal or aristocratic origins.

TOP TEN FILM POSTERS

You have to fight against being an antique
—Burt Lancaster

Vintage film posters are big business. The largest price ever achieved for a film poster was the $690,000 paid for the international version of Fritz Lang's iconic 1927 expressionist film *Metropolis*. It's an Art Deco masterpiece of graphic design by Heinz Schulz-Neudamm and is one of only four known to exist. In second place is the previous record holder, the poster for the 1932 film *The Mummy*, starring Boris Karloff, sold in 1997 for $435,500. In third place is a second *Metropolis* poster: the German titled three-sheet made for the domestic market, a snip at a mere $357,750 in 2000. The 1934 production *The Black Cat*, with Karloff and Bella Lugosi, comes in fourth – $334,600 in 2009. *The Bride of Frankenstein* muscles in at five; more Karloff here, the 1935 one-sheet fetching $334,600 in 2007. In sixth place is Lugosi starring in *Dracula*. Issued in 1931, the poster was owned by actor Nicholas Cage and sold for $310,700 when he parted with his collection in 2009. At number seven is another version of *The Black Cat* known as a 'style D', again 1934 and selling for $286,800 in 2007. Way down the list at number eight is *King Kong*, with a 'style A' design from 1933 which sold for $244,500 in 1999. That leaves a 1933 *Flying Down to Rio* at number nine, selling for £239,000 in 2008, and at ten is *Frankenstein, The Man Who Made a Monster*, with – you guessed who – Boris Karloff, selling for $198,000 in 1993. It was a record at the time.

STAR BORES

'*Star Wars* changed my life'. I'm sure many a 40-something has uttered those words but the fact is, for many of us it was true. I was thirteen when the film came out; I instantly fell in love with Princess Leia and have wielded several versions of Jedi lightsabers over the intervening decades. The Star Wars franchise has proved to be the ultimate merchandising opportunity, the big daddy of media-related marketing. It's commonplace to see Darth Vader or a Stormtrooper parading up and down the high street or at the local fête; it's part of our popular culture.

Pricing Star Wars material can be a nightmare but just like with rare comics, condition means everything. The Holy Grail for 'big bucks' collectors is the original figure of Darth Vader manufactured by Kenner. The first batch of small card-backed bubble-packed figures issued in 1978 had Darth with an extending lightsaber. This proved fragile and difficult to manufacture so was changed quickly. Examples of the original design can make as much as £4,000 in their original packaging or £1,000 loose.

So, with successive generations being wooed by the nostalgia of childish crushes and hairy wookies, the prices realised for original film-related articles and props sold over the years are pretty phenomenal. They include $104,000 for a blaster (gun) from the original film and £205,250 for a partial set of Stormtrooper armour sold by Christie's in 2011. A rare British quad cinema poster from 1977 could cost you £7,000–10,000.

May the force be with the merchandisers.

WHERE IS IT?

Have you ever visited a museum and chanced upon an unusual, moving or obscure historical object and been amazed that it is still in existence? Here are a few oddities that I've come across over the years – some more obscure than others.

Guy Fawkes' lantern. Housed at the Ashmolean Museum in Oxford, it was given to the university in 1641 by Robert Heywood, the son of the Justice of the Peace who was present at the arrest of Guy Fawkes.

Napoleon's toothbrush. On display at the Wellcome Collection, Euston, London, Napoleon's silver-gilt and horsehair toothbrush is engraved with an 'N' under a crown. Apparently, he used opium-based toothpaste.

The Spear of Destiny, also known as the Holy Lance, is the lance that pierced the side of Jesus while hanging on the cross. There have been several contenders over the centuries, the main one being the example displayed in the Imperial Treasury of the Hofburg Palace in Vienna, which has a long and fascinating history. It also contains an object that has been tested scientifically and is thought to be consistent with a 1st-century Roman nail.

Florence Nightingale's slippers. Another gem held in the vast collections of Henry Wellcome at the Wellcome Collection in London, the moccasins on display are said to have been worn by Florence while nursing in the Crimea.

Napoleon's hat from the battle of Waterloo. This claim goes to the military collections of the German Historical Museum in the Zeughaus (old arsenal) in Berlin. The hat, of black felt, has a folded fabric cockade of white, blue and red and was seized at the battle in 1815.

Charles Darwin's walking stick. This macabre ivory walking stick is topped with a carved skull with jewel inset eyes – quite apt for its former owner. See it at the Wellcome Collection.

Teeth pulled by Peter the Great. The Tsar of Russia from 1782 and renowned for his predilection for the macabre, Peter the Great's infamous anatomical collection is housed in his Wunderkammer in St Petersburg. One of the exhibits is a case of teeth pulled by the Tsar himself, who reputedly practised dentistry on whichever passer-by took his fancy.

The Duke of Wellington's boots. No doubt he had more than one pair, but the man renowned for giving us the 'wellington boot', Sir Arthur Wellesley, 1st Duke of Wellington, left a well-provenanced pair at his place of death, Walmer Castle in Kent. Also there is the chair in which he passed away.

General Montgomery's beret. Presented to him just before the battle of El Alamein in 1942, he donated it to the Bovington Tank Museum in Dorset in 1945.

Field Marshal Rommel's hat and goggles. Montgomery's adversary in the North African campaigns of the Second World War, Rommel's iconic 'look' was characterised by his hat and apparently American-made goggles. They can be seen in the Rommel Museum in his home town of Herrlingen, Germany.

AUCTION BIDDER

A Picasso is a Picasso, I don't mean to be
rude. But if there's weird stuff you know
nothing about you get fascinated
—Ayers Tarantino

If you've never been to auction then you are missing out. There are hundreds of them around the UK, ranging from the large international concerns such as Sotheby's and Christie's right down to small local auctions. There isn't anything you can't buy at auction, ranging from industrial plant, houses, cars, catering equipment to art and antiques. There's no great mystery to them; I've often heard people say that they're not for the public but this is simply not true. Auctions are open for everybody to buy and if you've got any sense you'll head down to your local saleroom and see what they've got on offer.

Buying at auction is rather like buying wholesale: in some instances, you can effectively cut out the middle-man and save money; all those old tales about scratching your nose and accidentally buying a Ming vase are largely untrue. These days you don't even have to set foot in the saleroom; you can bid online from the comfort of your own home, which saves you sitting in the saleroom all day waiting for few lots to 'come up'.

Personally, I like to view a sale. However good the online catalogue is, there is always more to see and more to fathom when you actually view a sale in person. The saleroom won't always get it right either, so part of the game is trying to divine something that they have missed or is more valuable to you as a collector or perhaps specialist dealer. Most salerooms offer a service for condition reports on the lots in the auction, which can be done over the telephone or online. However, opinions on condition can vary widely and it is sometimes quite difficult to get a totally accurate report; for that reason, I usually like to see the object. Certain artefacts are tactile and give you feedback only when you handle them – other people can't always convey that feeling to you.

It's also extremely important to look at things very carefully. Mistakes are easily made when viewing large amounts of objects; cracks and chips and restoration can easily go unnoticed. If you like an item but have no particular experience in that field then it's also good to study it with a critical eye; there may be a piece missing that you are unfamiliar with, which could drastically affect its value. I usually take the most pessimistic view and work towards the positive.

Beware, some auctions are notorious dumping grounds for unsold stock, restored items and, dare I say it, fakes, particularly the rash of cheap Chinese objects that regularly turn up. Some objects might also be loosely catalogued using the word '-style', as in 'Art Nouveau-style bronze figure', which can mean several things but in this case might imply that it is a modern reproduction. However, these are not always deceitful practices but often simply part of the jargon used in auctioneering terms, so be aware that some language may not be what you are used to.

General auctions containing several thousand lots will not describe every item or list damage, so it really is a case of buyer beware. However, for the seasoned auction-goer this is what it's all about. The staff may also be able to help you and unless you've discovered a lost Rembrandt in the sale and want to keep it close to your chest, don't hesitate to ask them for advice. Remember, you will have to pay buyer's commission, so factor this into your bidding. Standard rates range from around 15 to 20 per cent plus VAT.

When you've decided what you want to bid on, you can exercise several options. Firstly, you can go to the sale and bid in person. Most auction houses require you to register and will issue you with a paddle number to wave in the room. When bidding, keep calm, don't jump in hastily and remember that the auctioneer can only take two bids at once. There is no point trying to interject, he will come back to you if another bidder drops out. I tend to look as unconcerned as possible and usually hide behind a large piece of furniture or pillar. The assumption sometimes seems to be that if I am bidding on something it might be worth having, so lots of psychology comes into play in a saleroom. The auctioneer may also need to be 'read'; styles do vary. Don't be afraid to shout out if you think he has not seen you. A polite 'yes please sir' is generally the form.

Secondly, you can leave bids. This means writing your top bids down on a form and leaving the auctioneer to bid for you 'on the book'. This can be useful if you want to control the urge to get carried away in the frenzy of bidding, but some people don't like it because they have an inherent distrust of auctioneers and believe that they will always make you pay the top price – a practice called 'running up'. This has not been my experience over the years.

Thirdly, for more expensive items, you can book a telephone bid (or bids) and the auction house will ring you when the lot comes up. This is useful if you have no idea what you really want to pay and need to see what the room is dictating on the day, or you are after a 'sleeper' and you don't want to alert anyone. The chances are that someone else will have already spotted it but you never know. The tension and the anticipation are all part of it.

Lastly, you can sometimes bid online but be aware this service usually carries an additional fee of around 3 per cent on the hammer price.

If all of that advice works and you end up as the proud owner of a Georgian mahogany linen press then you might need to move it quite quickly before storage charges are applied. I find that polite, good communication with the porters and the saleroom can work wonders if things are delayed. And if you need a man and a van, the auction house will probably be able to recommend someone. Happy bidding!

Aqua fortis is the New Latin name for nitric acid, New Latin being the scholarly form used between c.1500 and 1900 ostensibly for scientific terms. It can sometimes be found in the form *aquaforti* at the bottom of antique etchings, indicating that it is an 'etched' image using 'strong water' – the literal meaning of the term. It is sometimes abbreviated to '*aq.*' or '*aquaf.*'.

STOLEN TO ORDER

An artist is somebody who produces things
that people don't need to have
—Andy Warhol

There have been many high-profile art thefts over the years, often from galleries and museums; perhaps one of the most publicised was that of Edvard Munch's iconic 'The Scream', stolen from the Munch Museum in Norway in 1994. It was recovered a few months later after a Scotland Yard/Getty Museum sting. Another version (there are four) was stolen from the same museum in 2004; it took until 2006 to find it. The only privately owned version was sold in 2012 by Sotheby's for a world-record US$120 million, so with the stakes this high it is little wonder that the world of organised crime takes an interest. Art theft is the third most lucrative criminal activity after drugs and arms.

The nature of the art and antiques business means that there has always been a demand for stolen artefacts, and it is a fact of life that stolen artefacts enter the market, often coming through convoluted channels, crossing borders and acquiring provenance and fake paperwork on the way. They are sometimes offered to collectors, dealers and auction houses who accept them as legitimate. Some objects emanate from conflict zones only to surface decades later and become the subject of heated debate about ownership. Art looted by the Nazis in the Second World War is a prime example and restitution cases are constantly being heard. It is estimated that the Nazis stole around 20 per cent of Europe's major art treasures. The mass movement of collections during the war to ensure their safety also led to artefacts 'going astray'.

The market for stolen Eastern antiquities is a particularly hard one to police and India has borne the brunt of illicit trading. South America is also a hotspot. Although there are rigid export rules, these seem to be easily circumvented by determined smugglers. The theft of deities from temples has been rife over the decades and in 2003 Sotheby's became embroiled in a major scandal when it came to light that they had been selling countless stolen Indian works of art supplied to them by an antiques dealer by the name of Vaman Ghiya. It transpired that he had a longstanding relationship with the auction house and that he employed a network of international object launderers who created a complicated paper trail while using petty thieves to steal deities and sculpture from poorly guarded temples and villages. Auction house catalogues featuring stolen works of art were found at his home.

This kind of theft is rife worldwide, spurred by high-stakes rewards and facilitated by poor people on the bottom rung for whom it is a way to put food on the table. However, it's the middlemen and end users that make the big profits and international crime-fighting organisations such as Interpol devote huge amounts of time and resources to chasing stolen art. In the UK the Art Loss Register is a central database against which individuals and institutions can research or list stolen artefacts. It works constantly with enforcement agencies to recover and repatriate lost works of art. Theoretically, it should nowadays be far more difficult to dispose of valuable artworks: communications are better, institutions, dealers and auction houses are more diligent. Hopefully thieves will eventually realise that some things are just too hot to handle.

A database was launched in 2010 by New York's Conference of Jewish Material Claims Against Germany in collaboration with the United States Holocaust Memorial Museum in Washington DC for individuals to search records of the Einsatzstab Reichsleiter Rosenberg (ERR), Hitler's agency that was set up to plunder and administer stolen artworks. It's estimated that there are over 650,000 items still to be repatriated.

Just a few of the most famous stolen works of art recovered and un-recovered:

The Amber Room. An entire carved amber room dating from 1701, stolen by the Nazis from the Catherine Palace near St Petersburg in 1941 and packed into 27 crates. It has never been recovered. A replica of the room has now been recreated.

The Mona Lisa by Leonardo da Vinci. Stolen from the Louvre in 1911 by Vincenzo Peruggia, it was recovered in 1913 when he tried to sell it. Estimated current value: £480 million.

The Boy in the Red Vest by Paul Cezanne. Stolen from the Foundation E.G. Bührle in Zürich in 2008; recovered in Serbia 2012. Estimated current value: £60 million.

The Just Judges by Jan Van Eyck. Stolen in 1934 by a Belgian called Arsène Goedertier, he took its whereabouts to his grave and it has never been recovered.

Portrait of a Young Man by Raphael. Stolen by the Nazis in Poland, it was included in Hitler's private collection. It has been missing since the end of the war but was reported in August 2012 as being in a secret bank vault, country unknown. Estimated current value: £65 million.

BACKSTAIRS BILLY

It may seem like a derogatory title but William Tallon was officially the Steward and Page of the Backstairs. He was the favourite servant of Queen Elizabeth, the Queen Mother. I met him many years ago, not long after the Queen Mother had passed away. I was called to the gate-house at Clarence House, William's home for many years while in her service. My brief was to help him with the imminent sale of some of his possessions, necessitated by his departure from his royally appointed house. I parked the car, just a few yards away from a guard wearing a bear-skin and it was with some trepidation that I knocked on the front door. As it flung open I was quickly ushered in by a slightly perturbed-looking, ruddy-faced man with wild hair who quickly proclaimed that he was being bothered by the press and it might be a good idea if I shielded my face. It soon became apparent why.

I immediately felt relaxed with William; he was charming and polite and immediately offered me his trademark 'drink', which, due to driving, I politely declined. He thrust a certain newspaper into my hand with a photograph of himself in a local launderette with words to the effect 'this is what it's come to', inferring that having to do your washing in this way was a mark of poverty. William showed me his tiny kitchen (the gatehouse was very small) and pointed out that there wasn't actually any room for a washing machine; in fact, he'd always used the launderette! He was unsurprisingly annoyed and intimated that if I wasn't careful I might be tomorrow's headline.

We sat down, chatted for over an hour and eventually spoke about the business of selling some of the contents of the gatehouse. Immediately, I was struck by his integrity in the matter. It was quite obvious to me as an auctioneer that the provenance and history of some of the items would be a valuable aid to boosting the prices at sale but he wanted none of that. In pointing out presents from the Queen Mother and the Queen he insisted that if they were offered for sale he did not want any attention drawn to them and that no unnecessary publicity should be attracted which might cause the Royal family discomfort. So that is exactly what happened: the items were sold with no hint as to their connection.

I made several visits to see William, both at the gatehouse and later at his flat in Kennington; on one visit I had to abandon my car after having a lunchtime drink but on no occasion did I find him anything other than a true gentleman who liked to chat. I found him fascinating. He passed away in 2007 and his chattels and personal papers were subsequently sold by Reeman Dansie auctioneers in 2008. These included a wonderful collection of royal memorabilia and ephemera. One letter that raised a cheer as it sold was a note from the Queen Mother reading 'I think that I will take two small bottles of Dubonnet and gin with me this morning, in case it is needed.' It realised £16,000.

HELEN OF TROY

Many years ago I met a Russian gentleman by the name of Igor. He had a particular interest in Oriental art and we became good friends over the course of our business. One evening I was drinking vodka and eating caviar with him and the conversation naturally came around to art and antiques, one of our favourite subjects. We started to talk about archaeology and I happened to mention the Schliemann treasure.

Heinrich Schliemann (1822–1890) was an eminent 19th-century archaeologist – although some might beg to differ on this description of his job title. Early pioneering archaeologists were essentially treasure hunters, so many of their practices are now considered careless or destructive. Schliemann excavated various sites, including Mycenae, where he discovered the famous 'mask of Agamemnon'.

The hill that he believed to be the ancient city of Troy in Anatolia is called Hissarlik and is actually a series of ancient cities dating from the Bronze Age to the Roman period. Schliemann's zealous excavation (including the use of dynamite) cut a huge swathe through the hill. In the process of excavating he came across a superb 'treasure', which he attributed to King Priam, together with many gold items and jewels which he called the 'jewels of Helen'

(Helen of Troy, that is). There's a famous photograph of Schliemann's wife Sophia wearing the jewels, which, incidentally, Schliemann smuggled out of the country. We now know, of course, that these were not correctly attributed in historical terms.

Some of the objects remained in Turkey and are now located in the Istanbul Archaeology Museum, but in 1881 the Royal Museums in Berlin acquired the other 'treasures' – which went missing at the end of the war from a secure bunker and were never seen again.

As I sipped more vodka I asked Igor if he knew anything about the treasure; he quite nonchalantly said, 'It's in Moscow; I've seen it in the State Archive.' I was flabbergasted. 'Just you wait and see,' he said, 'it will be revealed within the next few years.'

Sure enough, the treasure surfaced at the Pushkin Museum in 1993. It transpires that the Red Army had taken it from Berlin at the end of the war and the Soviet government had denied its existence ever since.

Igor sadly died many years ago. Time will tell whether the claims he made about various other artefacts prove to be correct.

WHAT'S A GRECIAN URN?

How can you impress your friends with your exemplary knowledge of Greek vase shapes? Amphora are simple but distinguishing a volute krater from a kalyx krater is a little more specialised. Here's an at-a-glance guide to the various shapes of vessels from the ancient world.

Amphora

Neck Amphora

Alabastron

Askos

Bell Krater

Column Krater

Kalyx Krater

Volute Krater

Kylix (two examples)

Kanthoros

Kyathos

Lebes
Gamikos

Deinos

Lekane

Lekythos

Loutrophoros

Lebes

Kotyle

Oenochoe (two examples)

Aryballos

Kalathos

Hydria

Pelike

Phiale Mesomphalos

Pithos

Psykter

Mastos

Pyxis

Skyphos

Stamnos

Olpe

HOW TO SPOT A FAKE

I once sold a rather fine pair of Georgian mirrors for a client. They made several thousand pounds at the auction and all parties were happy. About a year later I was thumbing through an auction catalogue for a sale in central London and there were the two mirrors. This wasn't an unusual occurrence in itself but as I read the description it became apparent that they now had a '19th century' pencil inscription on the back stating that they had come from a large stately home, which incidentally had burnt down in the 1960s. The inscription had been added fraudulently and had effectively doubled the value of the mirrors.

A quick phone call later and the mirrors were withdrawn; it was a remarkable instance of faking that didn't actually involve the manufacture of an object, rather, the fabrication of a lie. In essence, that's what all faking, counterfeiting and forging is: a fabricated lie. But there are many different ways to produce a fake and the provenance can be every bit as important as the object itself. That's why it is paramount not to take everything in the world of art and antiques at face value.

In a typical week I will see any number of fakes, whether I'm viewing an auction or visiting a client. The degrees of deception can be somewhat confusing. Alterations over time can render certain pieces of furniture 'fake' in some people's eyes; similarly, a 19th-century buffet constructed from parts of 17th- and 18th-century coffers can be called 'fake', when in fact it's little more than a Victorian flight of fancy, fashionably popular at the time. However, it is infuriating to view an auction and find a painting which at first glance looks a tempting 19th-century depiction of a Maori chieftain only to turn it over and find that it's a clever fake.

To be frank, my mantra is always be sceptical; if you are unsure then analyse the object carefully. I use a slightly perverse reverse logic to deconstruct an object. In the case of the Maori chieftain, the painting itself was quite well executed but a little 'over aged'; this was a prime subject for ethnographic collectors, yet it was placed in a small local saleroom, so alarm bells rang. As it was under glass and sealed, I was unable to see the back of the board it had been painted on; however, it was mounted in a 1960s glazed frame with a badly scrawled pencil note on the back: 'reframed 1966'. The paper parcel tape that sealed the reverse board onto the frame was particularly dirty with a 'washed' discoloration, far too dirty for the back of a frame that had been hung on a wall. The suspension string on the back also had traces of the same dirty wash, meaning that the colour had been applied with the string in situ. Also, the Phillips-head screws holding the string were powder-coated, indicating recent manufacture (although it shouldn't be assumed that Phillips screws in themselves are modern; they were invented in the 1930s), but enveloped by the parcel tape apparently applied in 1966. The dirt was particularly prevalent on the knots but not underneath them.

It took just a few seconds for me to realise that it was made to deceive. The clever deflective message on the back was merely to make a person accept that it had been reframed and not to question that aspect of the overall deceit. The fact is, you have to be careful; when it's 'buyer beware' it's essential to analyse things that look a little bit too good to be true with a highly critical eye, particularly when the subject is tempting. I didn't think the auction house was complicit in the deceit, but the picture was vaguely catalogued, suggesting they were unsure of its age. Paintings and art are a particularly interesting area when it comes to forgery; I cover this further elsewhere in the book (*see* Tom's Time Bombs, *page 139*).

Luckily, my experience as an auctioneer has given me a good grounding in this area and I've been fortunate enough (from a learning point of view) to be subjected to a whole plethora of fakes over the span of my career. That's not to say that I haven't made mistakes; I've been taken in on a few occasions and learnt a harsh lesson, each time making me wiser than the last.

As an auctioneer, dealer or collector, it's essential to be vigilant; battling the fakers is almost like fighting a cause. The Asian markets, especially China, have opened up the West to a plethora of fakes. A quick glance at eBay with the word 'netsuke' in the search window reveals a vast array of spuriously catalogued examples, many listed as '19th century' but patently modern, with colour washes applied; some are described as 'bone' when quite obviously they are made of resin. The problem is that these items rely on inexperienced buyers to make a face-value judgement.

Conversely, it's sometimes necessary to differenti-ate between fakes and reproductions because knowledge levels often dictate the difference between objects that are deliberate deceptions and those that are merely made 'in the style of'. Quite naturally, having spent over 25 years in antiques, I can quickly dismiss many things as reproductions but I've frequently been handed items on the *Antiques Roadshow* that the owners believe to be real. Scrimshaws are a case in point and I've seen countless decorative resin teeth 'engraved' with portraits of Nelson and decorated with pictures of HMS *Victory*; most are just too good to be true because real examples are so rare. These are not fakes, merely decorative reproductions. Wholesale cash-and-carry warehouses specialise in this type of material; trade buyers can wheel around a trolley and load up on all sorts of 'antique' items. And it's not uncommon to find such objects mixed in with antique and vintage items in shops and antique centres. The tags are often lacking in detail. I did once go into an antiques shop which from a distance had a tempting window, only to find that the entire premises were populated with cash-and-carry antiques. I politely asked where 'the old stuff was' and was met with short shrift.

Over the decades I've seen some clever attempts to cash in on fashionable items. Unusually coloured teddy bears were surfacing for a while but on closer inspection it was possible to see that they were old bears that had been dyed. Art Nouveau-style glass has flooded the market from Eastern Europe and China; copies of Gallé, Tiffany, Loetz and Lalique are not uncommon. One particular type of Gallé-style glass bears a lookalike signature but has an identifying name to denote it as a modern copy – I've seen this ground off. Even fake boxes can significantly increase the value of diecast or tin toys.

Some of my favourite fakes (if such a thing is allowed) are the Leica cameras that herald from Eastern Europe. I once filmed a fake 1936 Olympic Leica on the *Antiques*

Roadshow; the owner was not too pleased when I broke the news. Such fakes tend to be run-of-the-mill Leicas, or period Russian Leica-based copies such as Zorkis, that are later embellished to resemble more exclusive types of Leica. The deception stems from the much higher value of Leica cameras that were specially made for the Luftwaffe or German navy, or as short-run limited editions. Camera collectors are very familiar with these; they have been available for many years. In fact, they are regarded by the majority as just interesting reproductions, rather than deceitful fakes. All Leicas carry a serial number, so it's easy to check if you know where to look.

I'm only able to scratch the surface in these few paragraphs but don't let this put you off buying antiques; there are plenty of original, untainted pieces out there and lots of honest people waiting to sell them to you.

> Faking is by no means a new phenomenon and I have a particular interest in objects that are antique but purport to be even older. This can be an absolute minefield in areas such as antiquities and art but also very confusing when you might have to consider an Art Deco figure made in the 1960s revival period, which is only 30 years younger than it should be, but is poles apart in value. Never made as fakes, such things acquire age and patina over time making them difficult to tell apart.

TOM'S TIME BOMBS

Fraud is the daughter of greed
—Jonathan Gash

I would be the last person to condone the faking of objects and art for financial gain; however, I have to admit that I have occasionally harboured an admiration for craftsmen and artists who are adept enough to pull off the most incredible frauds. I suppose this mainly stems from the Robin Hood spirit of those that use their skill to take on the sometimes highbrow and supercilious experts and institutions that put themselves forward as the final word in art.

Perhaps the most famous art forger in the UK was Thomas Keating. Born in 1917, Tom worked after the war as an art restorer and artist; he struggled to make ends meet and also worked as a part-time decorator. Despite his skill, he found it difficult to become established as an artist in his own right and it's this struggle that undoubtedly contributed to his disenchantment with the art establishment. Keating decided to get his own back on what he perceived as greedy galleries making large profits at the expense of poor artists, and began to forge everything from Old Masters to Impressionists. He planted 'time bombs' in his works, employing techniques such as putting his signature on the canvas before painting, and then adding a layer of glycerine to the canvas, which would reveal the nature of the picture if restoration was undertaken.

Keating loved Rembrandt but also produced what he would have described as 'minor works' by other great artists such as Degas, Renoir, Fragonard and Gainsborough.

However, in 1970, it was noticed that there seemed to be a plethora of watercolours arriving at auction by the artist Samuel Palmer. When questions arose, Keating was forced to admit that they were his works and the cat was then firmly out of the bag. It's not known how many works Keating actually sold or placed on the market but he suggested himself that it was over 2,000. He was eventually arrested in 1977 and sent for trial but the case was dropped due to ill health and Keating won the heart of the people as a 'loveable rogue'. He later went on to produce a series of programmes for Channel 4, which are an amazing insight into his skill as an artist and the techniques he employed.

No one knows how many of Keating's works hang in galleries or private collections; more will no doubt be revealed in time, some too sensitive to be questioned perhaps? Interestingly, collecting Keating's work has become an area in its own right; once worthless, his paintings now have a notoriety and interest brought about by his skill and reputation as one of Britain's greatest art forgers. He died in 1984.

If you thought ultraviolet light was just for checking fake banknotes, making scorpions fluoresce in the dark and showing up women's underwear in 1980s discos then think again. A UV light is an indispensable piece of equipment for picture specialists as it has an uncanny ability to show up over-paint and alterations to paintings. This is particularly useful for detecting layers of historic restoration but also tampering and the addition of signatures, both of which, sadly, are all-too-common occurrences in the art world.

CHARITY CASE

Art is what you can get away with
—Andy Warhol

I recently came across the unusual case of Mark A. Landis, an American artist and forger who has specialised over the last twenty years or so in donating forged works to museums and institutions under the pretext of commemorating the death of his father.

Born in 1955, Landis was seventeen when his father died; this apparently affected him profoundly and he spent some time in a hospital where he was diagnosed as schizophrenic. He went to art school and made an unsuccessful foray into the art world with a gallery that unfortunately failed. He began to produce forgeries and donated them to over 50 museums and galleries in the United States, including smaller institutions that did not have the technical facilities to carry out exhaustive research. Pictures supposedly by Paul Signac and Louis Valtat were part of his repertoire. He even donated versions of the same picture to different institutions using the persona of a Jesuit Father as a disguise.

Eventually, in 2007, he aroused suspicion when he gave several works to the Oklahoma City Museum of Art. An investigation took place and when all the dots had been joined it was obvious that he had given a sizable collection of works away, though some were merely well-executed over-coloured photocopies. No charges have ever been brought against Landis and an exhibition of his work was held in 2012, organised by the main protagonists of his detection. It was titled 'Faux Real'. Apparently Landis lent the exhibition his Jesuit costume.

PROVENANCE IS EVERYTHING

It took me four years to paint like Raphael,
but a lifetime to paint like a child
—Pablo Picasso

This is the fascinating tale of how a thoroughly dishonest man named John Drewe and an impoverished artist called John Myatt defrauded around £1.8 million by creating provenances on forged works of art. As everyone knows, provenance is everything, particularly with valuable pictures. Drewe, born in 1948, had spent most of his life masquerading as a physicist in various countries, institutions and schools. In 1985 he persuaded Myatt to paint 'copies', paying him a fraction of what they were to later sell for. Drewe cleverly aged the pictures with dirt and vacuum cleaner dust, and many were subsequently sold through Christie's and Sotheby's. The ingenious part of the fraud was to create provenances for the works by infiltrating major archival sources trusted by the British art establishment. This he did by making donations to the Tate Gallery and forging references to gain entry to archives at the Victoria and Albert Museum. He then proceeded to create a fake paper trail to give the forged works substance by making false insertions in catalogues, forging bills of sale and bribing people to sign documents saying that they had previously owned the pictures.

In 1995, Drewe was eventually imprisoned after Myatt agreed to help the police with their enquiries. It is thought it will take years to find all the forged material that Drewe planted in various archives. As for the pictures, many are undoubtedly still regarded as the real McCoy.

A FAMILY BUSINESS

When you look at art made by other people,
you see what you need to see in it
—Alberto Giacometti

In Scotland Yard's own words, Shaun Greenhalgh and his family were 'possibly the most diverse forgery team in the world, ever'. Theirs was a scandal that rocked the world of art and museums when it transpired that an unqualified former antiques dealer and his family had been defrauding the art world for seventeen years between 1989 and 2006 with a series of varied and audacious fakes that ranged from ancient stone carvings to paintings and 20th-century sculpture. When police eventually raided the unassuming house near Bolton, they found a veritable selection of materials, tools and paperwork that the Greenhalghs had used to create the objects and their fake provenances. The most publicised pieces included the 'Amarna Princess', an alabaster statue executed in the Egyptian 'Amarna' style dating from around 1350BC and depicting one of the daughters of the Pharaoh Akhenaten and Queen Nefertiti.

Shaun's family had formed a tight-knit team which used snippets of family history and his father George's old age and infirmity as a naïve front for passing off the items. It worked well. The 'Amarna Princess' acquired a provenance showing that it had been bought by Shaun's grandfather at the 1892 Silverton Park sale of the 4th Earl of Egremont as part of a suitably ambiguous lot of 'eight Egyptian Figures'. It was authenticated by the British Museum and Christie's and sold to the Bolton Museum for over £400,000.

Other clever deceptions included one based on the Risley Park Lanx, a large Roman silver dish found in 1729 and then broken. Its subsequent disappearance left behind no more than sketches and references, which Shaun exploited to create a version of the Lanx fabricated from real melted-down Roman silver coins. Its analysis threw up various anomalies and queries but it was loosely accepted as a contemporary version and sold for £100,000 by Sotheby's. Two American benefactors purchased the piece and then donated it to the British Museum, where it was put on display.

The Greenhalghs were eventually caught when they tried to pass off three Assyrian reliefs purportedly from Nineveh. Unfortunately for the family, despite the British Museum initially verifying the authenticity of the plaques, a specialist at Bonham's auctioneers spotted inconsistencies and a glaring spelling mistake in the cuneiform script came to light. Shaun had actually bought the stone from a mason in Wiltshire. Their fate was sealed and, some months later, the Greenhalghs were arrested.

As with many forgers, it is thought that the motivation for the Greenhalghs' counterfeiting spree was not necessarily monetary. They did not lead an extravagant lifestyle and their council house was reported as being 'relatively frugal' and 'shabby'. Shaun's lack of recognition as an evidently talented artist may have been part of the reason; a desire to hoodwink the establishment is so often mooted as being a cause for such behaviour. Many institutions tried to distance themselves from the debacle, saying in retrospect that Shaun's talent was limited, but public opinion largely sided with a sympathetic view of the family. One figure of a pottery faun had even been exhibited in a major Gaugin exhibition at the Art Institute of Chicago. In many ways, Shaun's story seems like a sad case of misused skill. No one is really quite sure how many Greenhalgh fakes are still out there.

Shaun's shed was recreated for an exhibition at the V&A in 2010 as part of an exhibition on art forgery in conjunction with the Metropolitan Police. Several of his fakes were exhibited, including the 'Amarna Princess'.

WOODEN PUZZLE

The artist versus the establishment; it's a common theme in the creative world and a tussle in which the sculptor Brian Willsher found himself embroiled when he locked horns with the Inland Revenue in the 1960s.

Willsher's distinctive wooden sculptures have gained a considerable following over the years; their exploded interlocking abstract designs have become must-have items for interior designers. Born in 1930, Willsher began his wood-sculpting career in the 1950s, initially selling bowls and lamp bases to Heals and Liberty. His experimentation with abstract forms, using an adapted band saw, gathered momentum. His work was accepted and shown by galleries as sculpture but in 1968 the Inland Revenue refused to classify his work as art, meaning it was subject to a 40 per cent manufacturer's tax levied on household decorations.

Major artists came out in his defence, including Henry Moore. The *Guardian* published an article entitled 'When is a sculpture not a sculpture?' and criticised the Revenue for its 'insidious claim' that the 'ornamental qualities' of his work were precisely what made it taxable. Willsher himself retaliated by showing a piece at the Royal Academy of Arts with a low £50 price tag on it – whereupon his Brooke Street Gallery disowned him for devaluing his work.

Willsher won the case but afterwards, as a result of all the media attention, he shunned the limelight, continuing to produce his sculptures in south London while mainly selling from market stalls. Exhibitions of his work have been intermittent but he did show in the 1980s and 90s. He died in 2010 but his sculpture continues to grow a cult following among collectors.

'Treen' is the collective term used for small wooden objects such as spice boxes, nutcrackers, love spoons and snuffboxes. The word originates from the Old English *treōw* for tree or wood. Birmingham City Art Gallery has a collection of over 7,000 such items that once belonged to the scholarly collector Edward Pinto (1901–1972). He wrote what is considered to be the definitive book on the subject.

FIVE-CLAWED DRAGONS

The dragon is a legendary and culturally important creature in China and throughout Asia. In folklore and myth it symbolises power and strength and was adopted as a potent symbol of the Emperor's authority. The imperial throne is known as the 'Dragon Throne'. But what is the difference between a dragon painted with five claws as opposed to one with four claws? Well, Chinese art is constructed according to a very specific hierarchy. In the Zhou Dynasty (1046–256BC), five claws denoted it as fit for an Emperor ('The Son of Heaven'). Nobles had to make do with four claws, ministers with three.

The latent power of the dragon continued to be emphasised throughout various dynasties by its special attributes; the 'Long' dragon in particular, with five toes, sometimes depicted in colours, was reserved expressly for the Emperor and his close family and relatives. The misuse of the motif in any form, be it toe number or colour, was considered treason and was punishable by death – of the whole clan, that is!

The market for Chinese works of art has seen a meteoric rise in recent years with objects making increasingly unpredictable amounts of money. Imperial porcelain that just a few decades ago was worth thousands can now realise millions, but the market is still quite fickle and there are various characteristics that naturally make some pieces far more valuable than others. A vase with some of those magical attributes (e.g.

five claws) was sold by Tennants Auctioneers in Yorkshire in 2012. The 17th-century blue and white vase that was literally 'touched' by the Emperor came with a price tag of £2.6 million.

Other highly valued characteristics include the use of the number nine. This is an auspicious number in China and it is typical to see it employed in various aspects of art; it was regarded as the Emperor's number and that's why imperial Chinese palaces and gardens are often decorated with features known as 'Nine Dragon Walls'. Only the most senior of officials were allowed to wear robes embroidered with dragons, and even then they had to be covered with a surcoat; the Emperor would wear a robe with nine embroidered dragons but would cover one out of respect.

Colour is also important in Chinese art. Yellow (or gold) is an imperial colour and denotes objects associated with the Emperor or his court. In the great Qing Dynasty (1644–1912) only the Emperor could officially wear yellow or 'gold' but his bodyguards were permitted to wear it while in his presence. The Emperor would award a yellow jacket known as *ma gua* or 'riding jacket' as a way of bestowing the highest honour on a person. Yellow is also used in Chinese ceramics in the same way.

Various other edicts enforced throughout history have variously forbidden commoners from wearing clothing depicting white rabbits, written characters depicting fortune or longevity and male phoenixes.

In light of the new Chinese billionaire art-collecting class, it is perhaps little wonder that such royal rarities are today making so much money.

POISON CHALICE

Mercury sulphide or cinnabar is a highly toxic mineral processed as a pigment and used in many cultures dating as far back as 8,000 years (not unlike its poisonous acquaintance red lead or lead oxide). Its distinctive bright orange or red hues have been used in both ritualistic and practical ways by the ancient Chinese and in South American cultures such as Moche and Inca. Its use for everything from painting ceramics to tattooing and sprinkling in burials has ensured that it constitutes a significant hazard to archaeologists.

Its extraction since ancient times in various parts of South America has caused major ongoing pollution problems over many centuries. Extraction of mercury from the ore – required for refining in the silver and gold mining industries – has also been responsible for much pollution.

Chinese cinnabar lacquer-ware was thought to have originated in the Song Dynasty (960–1279) and is sometimes flagged as potentially noxious; however, the mercury sulphide is trapped within the lacquer and so poses little threat unless broken. I'm sure this was not the same situation for those that made it. Superlative cinnabar boxes can be worth thousands.

EMPIRE CRUNCH

The humble biscuit – who would have thought it such an important factor in the building of the British Empire? During the Victorian period, biscuits became an export and expedition staple and factories such as Huntley & Palmers, founded in 1822, became synonymous with the power of global branding. Based in Reading, the company pioneered the early use of tins, particularly the large square 7lb and 10lb examples, which preserved the biscuits and enabled them to find their way to every corner of the globe. At its height, the company had over 5,000 employees and exported 10 per cent of its production to India. Reading was known as 'biscuit town'.

Huntley & Palmers were also marketing-savvy and cleverly introduced the idea of novelty packaging; their colourful lithographed tins, ranging in shape from sentry boxes to delivery vans, became highly collectable. Some of these tins can realise hundreds of pounds among collectors, with some 400 designs made between 1868 and the outbreak of the Second World War.

And what of the biscuits themselves? It might seem strange to think of them becoming collectors' items but their historical associations have indeed seen them appear in high-profile auctions. Henry Stanley set off in search of Dr Livingstone laden with supplies of Huntley & Palmers biscuits. Captain Robert Falcon Scott took specially formulated energy-rich biscuits on the expedition to the South Pole, but in an age where little was known about vitamins, Scott and his men, despite their special biscuits, were left highly deficient of Vitamins B and C. Amundsen, his rival in the race to the pole, survived on a vitamin-rich Norwegian-style diet of seal and penguin meat. His biscuits were baked with oatmeal and yeast, rather than white flour and sodium bicarbonate; again, they were much more nutritious than Scott's. Tins of perfectly preserved Huntley & Palmers biscuits can still be found at Scott's hut at Cape Evans to this very day. Fellow explorer Ernest Shackleton's hut at Cape Royds remains in a similar state of preservation – biscuits included – and both are now protected sites.

Any souvenirs related to heroic British explorers garner great interest among collectors. A biscuit from Shackleton's Antarctic expedition of 1907–9 sold for £1,250 in 2011. In 1999, Christie's sold a Huntley & Palmers biscuit from Scott's tent; it was a potent and poignant symbol of all that is best about British endeavour but tinged with an air of sadness. It was purchased by the explorer Sir Ranulph Fiennes for £4,000.

THE BIDDENDEN MAIDS

Still on the subject of biscuits, I once purchased a mixed lot of objects at auction which contained an interesting-looking 'biscuit' (for want of a better description). I had no idea what the item was but later discovered that the biscuit, described by the Pitt Rivers Museum as 'memorial food', is a strange memento of a custom that has persisted in the village of Biddenden in Kent since the 16th century.

Depicted on the thick flour-and-water 'cake' are the naïve images of two women, Eliza and Mary Chulkhurst, who have the strange honour of being recorded as the earliest known conjoined twins in Britain. The twins by all accounts gifted around 20 acres of land for charitable causes, which every year continue to provide what is known as the 'Biddenden dole'. Every Easter Monday, bread, cheese and beer were distributed to the poor of the parish, but by all accounts, by the 17th century the situation had become somewhat riotous with people arriving from far and wide in the hope of free food, beer and the famous 'biscuits'. The church, who administered the charity, attempted to curtail it, however, their protestations were legally overruled and the custom still takes place every year, favouring around 60 or so local people with a 'dole' of bread, cheese, butter and tea. They also receive a 'biscuit', some of which are sold to inquisitive tourists.

The biscuits themselves have a purely commemorative function these days but are identifiable in style from the different moulds used over their several-hundred-year history. The one I acquired is identical to the example in

The Biddenden Maids

the Pitt Rivers collection and dates from around 1900. Despite the biscuits being of relatively little monetary value, Eliza and Mary have left us the legacy of a medieval custom that continues to persist to this day.

THE RARITY OF CATS

Are you a cat person or a dog person? Cats have had a chequered past, their lure varying widely through history and from culture to culture. They have always been appreciated for their vermin-control qualities and we know that they were venerated by the ancient Egyptians. However, in other epochs and particularly in European culture, cats have been depicted as heretical or in league with the devil, a view that was particularly prevalent in the Middle Ages when they were routinely killed or culled. Cat superstitions, particularly black cats, are still part of our folklore and it's routine to joke about witches and how it's unlucky for a black cat to cross your path.

Unfortunately the bad press lingered well into the 18th century and for this reason cats are quite poorly represented in European art. Dogs, of course, have long had a place in man's home both as working animals and as pets, and are well represented in art – think of all those Staffordshire spaniels that graced Victorian mantelpieces. But have you ever seen any cats of the same period? They are very rare – and with rarity comes greater value.

By the late 18th century, increasing urbanisation had given cats a greater raison d'être. Their vermin-control capabilities came to the fore and their reputation was gradually rehabilitated. By the early 19th century cats were being kept as pets – but it wasn't until the mid-Victorian period that cats became popular in advertising.

In 1871 the first cat show was held at the Crystal Palace in London. Early pottery cats tend to be quite amusing representations of 'moggies'. Examples by Obadiah Sherratt (1780–1840) are much sought after; most of these are unmarked and only attributable by style and knowledge. An 18th-century example could cost you several thousand pounds!

The *trembleuse* was a wonderful 18th-century innovation and one that should be reinvented for the modern market. It's basically a cup and saucer, the saucer of which has either a significantly raised gallery or a deep depression in the centre, into which the cup snugly fits. The name comes from the French for 'to tremble', and these items are always associated with saving jittery old folk from spilling their precious tea, but frankly, I think it's just a good straightforward way of keeping your cup on the saucer.

BRANDED

Advertising material is highly collectable. It's a diverse field with plenty of ephemera and objects to choose from including enamelled signs, shop counter displays, branded cabinets, magazine advertisements and promotional items, to name but a few. Certain brands have endured and there's a great nostalgia for old favourites such as Marmite, OXO, Camp Coffee and Tate & Lyle syrup. These products have remained very loyal to their original brand image, which has given them an iconic status in terms of advertising and brand recognition. The oldest brand in British retail history is Pears soap. First registered in 1789 by Andrew Pears, it's the world's oldest brand name, making Pears transparent soap the longest continually selling branded product on the planet.

Pears set up his factory near Oxford Street in London and his training as a barber gave him a good understanding of the cosmetic requirements of his clientele. Most of the products then available were harsh, using ingredients such as arsenic to produce the sallow white complexions that were so fashionable in the period. Pears' recipe was based on glycerine and natural ingredients, and the translucence of the soap proved to be an advantageous marketing novelty.

Interestingly, the company became equally famous for its advertising material and is lauded as a founding force in the world of product promotion. In addition to winning various international medals in recognition of its soap, Pears employed famous artists of the day such as Sir John Everett Millais, who produced 'Bubbles', one of the most iconic advertising images ever. Painted in 1886 and originally entitled 'A Child's World', the painting was purchased by Thomas Barrett, the managing director of Pears, and altered – apparently with the permission of Millais – to include the soap and wording. The use of the picture prompted a heated debate between the relationship of art and advertising. The young boy in the picture was Millais' grandson and the painting, like many works of art, had a hidden message. The bubbles were actually emblematic of the fragility of life, the potted plant was emblematic of life itself and the broken plant pot suggested death. Critics at the time accused Millais of prostituting his art for commercial purposes. Rather out of fashion these days, an original lithograph of 'Bubbles' can be purchased at auction for as little as £20. The original painting can be seen at the Lady Lever Art Gallery, in Port Sunlight.

Other clever promotional gimmicks included counter-stamping coins with 'Pears Soap'. These were often French coins and were even accepted as penny equivalents! Although collectable, they are fairly common and can be purchased for a few pounds each. These days, the Pears brand is owned by Unilever and the product manufactured in India. Sadly, the formula has been altered and the distinctive smell has changed. True to the modern age, a Facebook campaign was launched to restore the original formula; alas, it has not been done as yet. The brand endures but the charm may well have been lost.

FAKE OR FORTUNE FOUND?

The aim of art is to represent not the outward appearance of things, but their inward significance
—Aristotle

He's the master sleuth of the art world and the perfect example of how the thrill of the chase and the process of discovery can be such an enthralling and rewarding process. Philip Mould OBE is regarded as one of the foremost specialists in his field, dealing in British art and Old Masters from his Dover Street Gallery in London. He's also regarded as the UK's leading expert in British portraiture and forms a formidable team with his colleague Dr Bendor Grosvenor in tracking down, researching and restoring lost works by great masters.

He is, in effect, the man that the auction houses are least happy to see, generally based on the assumption that he may well be chasing a work that they haven't spotted or managed to correctly pin down. This is of course largely what the antiques and art world is all about: that extra knowledge, that skill to divine and that passion to pursue and see through a picture to the end. Philip's unabashed no-nonsense attitude to challenging the traditional art establishment makes him both a champion of artistic causes, ever determined to prove his point, and also the antithesis of the staid, old-fashioned curatorial style that still seems unswerving in its opposition to suggestion or analysis of artistic résumés.

His television series *Fake or Fortune*, with *Antiques Roadshow* presenter Fiona Bruce, has shown the belligerence that even a specialist like Philip encounters in the art market, but it's an absolutely fascinating insight into the processes of proving (or not) that a work is by a particular hand. By peeling back the layers, known works have revealed fabulously startling provenances and fascinating information. The financial rewards can be high, the satisfaction of restoring lost masterpieces to their rightful place in history immense.

Philip and his team have brought restitution to some of the biggest names in art history: Gainsborough, Van Dyke, Constable and Hogarth, to name but a few. His discoveries, gracing some of the most distinguished galleries and museums of the world, add weight to his much-recognised endeavours.

STEP INTO HISTORY

Imagine using a carved stone slab in your garden as a step, only to find that it's a rare 1,000-year-old 'Temple Moonstone', or granite semi-circular step from a Sri Lankan temple. That would be news enough but then imagine sending it for auction with a £20,000–30,000 estimate – even better. Such a situation unfolded in England early in 2013, and on 23 April the stone sold for £553,250 … a little over the estimate!

The richly carved slab had been brought to England by William Murdoch Thyne, a Scottish civil engineer. He had worked on several engineering projects in Sri Lanka (Ceylon) between 1915 and 1937. The step had been installed in his garden at Brackenhill in Crowborough, Sussex.

Bonham's auctioneers had extensively researched the piece, which evidently had come from the ancient city of Anuradhapura. Stories abounded in the press about which auction houses and which television shows had 'turned it down'. In reality, an advance party for the *Antiques Roadshow* had said they thought it very interesting but logistically far too difficult to dig out of the garden and transport to the show, a little different to the inflexion that it was 'turned down'.

The story illustrates once again that with many rare objects you often never know their true value until you sell them.

DESIGN ICONS

I don't want to be interesting, I want to be good
—Ludwig Mies van der Rohe

Take the humble chair. In reality, it's little more than an object for sitting on, a place to park your posterior, a place to wait, a place to work or a place to relax, but despite the simplicity of its rationale, the chair has occupied and obsessed some of the brightest minds in the history of design, architecture and psychology, spawning whole ideologies, design movements and revolutionary advances and applications in modern materials. From the humblest forest-made 'turner's' chair to the truly revolutionary, the chair has become much bigger than the sum of its parts; it is the basis for some of the most iconic designs ever made.

So what makes a design iconic? There are various factors: groundbreaking designs that have become part of the international language of style and design iconography often materialised within the midst of conventional thinking, polarising established thought with unsurpassed originality or use of materials. Dutch designer Gerrit Rietveld's 'Red/Blue chair' of 1918/1923 was like little else before it, a 3D Mondrian-style construction, not suited to comfort but groundbreaking in concept. No design book would be complete without it.

Ludwig Mies van der Rohe's 'Barcelona Chair' (1929); Marcel Breuer's 'Wassily' (1925–27); the 'No. 670' and 'No. 671', chair and ottoman designed by Charles and Ray Eames, beloved of architects – these are chairs that have made their mark in history. Originals can be expensive but most have been produced under licence for decades and value often depends on the licensee and the period in which they were reissued.

In 2009 at the Christie's sale of the contents of Yves Saint Laurent's apartment in Paris, a unique 'Dragons' armchair (1917–19) by Eileen Gray made a staggering €22 million. A favourite one to quote, and far more affordable, is the humble 'Polyprop' designed by British designer Robin Day in 1962. Without doubt, you are certain to have sat on one, probably without realising that you were using an iconic piece of design. These injection-moulded stacking chairs with metal legs, so beloved of church halls, are the best-selling seat in the world at over 18 million units. You can buy them second hand for a few pounds each.

Personally my favourite chair is the sinuous and beautifully crafted 'Chieftain' (1949) by Danish designer Finn Juhl; but whether your tastes are Scandinavian, American Mid-century Modern or Pop, there's an iconic design out there waiting for you to park your posterior on – after all, that's what they're made for.

Barcelona

Wassily

Chieftain

Polyprop

'Dragons'
armchair

Red/Blue
chair

No. 670
(chair)
and 671
(ottoman)

LUGGAGE LABEL

Louis Vuitton – it's a brand synonymous with luxury and style. If you were setting off on a European tour in the late 19th century you would undoubtedly be laden down with all manner of baggage. The variety available included names lost to us these days, items such as 'square mouth' bags, 'knockabout bags', 'brief bags' and 'carriage bags', all made in a variety of skins ranging from crocodile, walrus and pigskin to the more common cow hide. However, a Louis Vuitton trunk would have been an expensive item even then. Founded in 1854, the company grew to be one of the biggest global brands. Nowadays, early model trunks in the light brown and beige canvas stripe that was introduced in around 1876 (the iconic *LV* trademark appeared later) are popular with interior designers, and make very good coffee tables. Christie's auctioneers sold a particularly good example in February 2013 for £30,000.

ETIQUETTES DE VINS

We all know that wine is a highly collectable investment commodity; certain vintages can be worth large amounts of money. I recall being very disappointed on opening a highly collectable 1985 Romaneé-Conti La Tâche – it was like vinegar! At current prices, had I left it corked, that same bottle would be worth in the region of £1,000. I kept the bottle for a few days, sulked then threw it out. A recent delve around the internet was very enlightening. Interestingly I found empty Romaneé-Conti bottles for sale and also found several articles on the counterfeit wine market, including fake bottles of Château Lafite originating from China. There's obviously a market for refilling old bottles with cheap wine. It seems that where there are collectors and high stakes involved, people will go to just about any lengths to cash in or exploit their fellow human beings.

Saving the label from the bottle would have been a legitimate measure. Collecting wine labels is a very popular hobby and my La Tâche label would have had great appeal. Personally, I'm very much a fan of traditional-looking French labels: red, gold and black on a white background with a picture of a château; however, certain great houses such as Mouton Rothschild have a reputation for commissioning or utilising works by some of the world's greatest artists on their labels, including Picasso, Lucian Freud and Jeff Koons. Collectors do however have one major complaint – modern glues make it very difficult to remove them.

If you thought it was all about the contents of the bottle, then think again.

THE PRESIDENT'S TIPPLE

Hardy Rodenstock is perhaps the most infamous and high-profile wine collector and dealer in the world. His legendary wine tastings in the 1990s involved hundreds of rare wines dating from the 18th century onwards. In 1985 he acquired several bottles of rare 18th-century wine that had apparently been discovered in a walled-up cellar in Paris. They were engraved with the initials of the American president Thomas Jefferson, a well-known wine collector who spent considerable time in France in the 18th century. A bottle engraved '1787 Lafitte Th. J' was offered for sale at Christie's auctioneers in New York, 1987, where it realised £105,000, still the highest sum ever paid for a single bottle of wine. It was bought by Christopher Forbes of the Forbes Empire.

Several bottles were sold by other auction houses but suspicions were raised sometime later when Bill Koch, who purchased some of the wine, wanted to exhibit the bottles at the Boston Museum of Fine Arts. Investigations into the provenance produced sketchy results and analysis of the wine and the bottles revealed that the engraving on the glass had been executed with an electric power tool. The wine has been the subject of ongoing lawsuits ever since. In Benjamin Wallace's 2009 book *The Billionaire's Vinegar*, scientific tests conducted on the wine gave a date of 1962.

The toddy lifter is the ultimate quiz object; few people outside of the world of antiques guess its purpose when confronted with an example. The toddy lifter is an ingenious and yet very simple way of transferring liquid (generally alcohol) from a bowl into a glass and consists of a hollow elongated glass bulb-like object (usually with cut decoration) with a hole in the top of the flanged neck and a hole drilled through the ovoid reservoir. You simply put the bulbous reservoir into the punch bowl, let it fill, put your finger over the top hole – creating a vacuum that prevents the liquid trickling out – and lift over to the glass. Upon releasing your finger the drink naturally drops into the glass. Genius! Collectors love them.

HITLER'S DIARIES

It was the discovery of the century, one that could have rewritten the history books, but it turned out to be an elaborate hoax perpetuated by Konrad Kujau, a notorious forger from Stuttgart. *Stern* magazine's headline in 1983 announcing the discovery of Hitler's diaries caused a worldwide media frenzy. The 60 volumes were said to have been rescued from an aeroplane crash in 1945, but the 9 million marks paid by *Stern* for the diaries and other supporting material was to prove a very poor investment. The initial analysis of the diaries was not thorough enough and despite using reputable and authoritative experts to help with authentication, serious mistakes were made in hastily bringing the diaries to the world media before the content had been properly investigated.

It transpired that much of the material had simply been copied from published works; scientific tests on the diaries proved the ink and paper to be modern; and in retrospect, despite having been shown to specialists, the handwriting bore few similarities to that of Hitler. The resultant fallout saw the resignation of several high-level publishing executives. As often seems to be the case, the desire to make a groundbreaking discovery can often cloud the facts; a bit of greed and some vanity will usually complete the mix – it's what fakers and forgers rely on.

Although it was the Hawker Hurricane that initially bore the brunt of the Battle of Britain, it was the Supermarine Spitfire that became the symbol of the RAF's struggle against the Luftwaffe.

The result of this mythical status is that they are now highly collectable. No longer will you find them balanced outside RAF bases on pedestals; they are now far too valuable and were replaced with fibreglass replicas long ago.

There are thought to be around 50 flying examples in the world, owned by museums and wealthy collectors. Their value: around £2 million each.

THE GANG OF FIVE

Forbidden Planet, released in 1956, is in real terms one of the most expensive films ever made. It was a groundbreaking cinematic science fiction masterpiece and featured stylish and extensive sets, effects never seen before – and Robby the Robot, cinema's first mechanical character that didn't look like a tin can. Robby alone cost $125,000. The film was highly successful and won an Academy Award for the special effects; however, the star of the show was really Robby and the film fuelled the growing love of futuristic design and toys, particularly space toys.

In the post-war period, Japanese companies had to diversify quickly and one area in which they excelled was the production of tinplate mechanical toys. These are now highly collectable and robots are pretty well at the top of the tinplate collecting tree.

The first tinplate robot made by KT in Japan was a rather simple, small clockwork figure in yellow, called Lilliput. Thought to have been made circa 1938–41 (precise dates are sketchy), he's very collectable and worth around £3,000 in good condition. Beware of fakes – there are plenty on the internet.

Atomic Robot Man (A.R.M.) from 1949 is also very sought after, particularly with the very rare derivation stencilled on his back, 'Souvenir of the New York Science Fiction Conference'; there are only three known examples.

Following the immediate success of *Forbidden Planet*, manufacturers were quick to pick up on Robby and it's not uncommon to see examples of robots that closely resemble him; licensing wasn't quite as rigid as it is today. Nomura's 'Robby Space Patrol' vehicle is extremely sought after and you'll receive little change from £2,000 for a reasonable example.

Top of the list for serious robots collectors are a group of 'metal sardine boxes' known as the 'Gang of Five'. Made by Masudaya in the 1950s, a full set of these awkward-looking chaps are regarded as the holy grail of the robot-collecting world. Six were originally planned but five were eventually produced: Sonic (Train) Robot, Non-Stop (Lavender) Robot, Target Robot, Machine Man and Radicon Robot complete a very expensive line-up.

Condition is always an issue with tinplate and the battery compartments are notoriously prone to corrosion from leaking cells. Machine Man is actually the rarest and in December 2012 an example sold for $45,600 at Morphy Auctions in Pennsylvania, USA. The other four partners in crime, all the property of one collector, realised $10,800 for Radicon, $10,200 for Target, $8,400 for Sonic and $7,200 for Non-Stop. Another showstopper was a Nomura Robby lookalike that made $10,200. Past visions of the future so often form the collectables of the now.

A COMPLETE MONOPOLY

It's the best-selling game in history and it's thought that at least 250 million editions of Monopoly have been sold since 1935. The earliest references to the board game date from around 1903 when an American lady, Elizabeth Phillips, developed a game entitled 'The Landlord's Game'. It was self-published and various versions of her idea were adopted and revised by numerous people until a version appeared in 1934 that formed the basis for the edition issued by Parker Brothers in 1935, the standard set we all know today.

Charles Darrow, a heater salesman from Philadelphia, has taken much of the credit for the design of the game; he patented it in 1935 and then sold Parker Brothers the rights. They initially turned it down but reconsidered when they saw Darrow's success in self-promoted sales to department stores. Within a year they were producing 20,000 sets a week. Darrow became the first board-game millionaire.

Monopoly continues to be a bestseller and over the decades has been licensed the world over. Special-edition formats include deluxe versions, film-related versions and even a new branded 'Here and Now' edition which uses a Toyota Prius, a Starbucks coffee cup and an order of McDonalds french fries as some of the counters.

Values on the whole are fairly low for old sets; the production figures tell you why – they simply aren't rare. However, a rather scrappy-looking set recently turned up on the *Antiques Roadshow*, replete with evidence tags; it was the set used by the Great Train Robbers to while away the time in their hideout while waiting for things to calm down after the robbery. Apparently, there was one difference in their game: they used real money instead of the standard-issue Monopoly notes!

CARD SHARP

Known as the T206 Honus Wagner, the most expensive cigarette card in the world depicts a player from the Pittsburgh Pirates baseball team called, naturally, Honus Wagner. He is regarded by many as one of the best baseball players in history. The card was issued by the American Tobacco Company between 1909 and 1911 but Wagner was concerned about children buying cigarettes to obtain the card so he refused to let ATC continue to issue it. The result was that only 60–200 were thought to have made it into circulation. The most famous of these cards is the 'Gretzky T206 Honus Wagner', which has worked its way through a succession of owners, including Wayne Gretzky of ice hockey fame. In 1933 the card was listed as being worth $50; in 2007 it was sold for $2.8 million.

The impulse to collect has provided the basis for children's games going back generations, not least the Pokémon phenomenon of recent years. The most expensive Pokémon card is known as the Pikachu 'Illustrator'. Valued at $20,000, it was given away as a competition prize and only four are thought to exist – so don't worry too much about flicking through the dog-eared pile in your child's bedroom.

CEREAL KILLER

Were you one of those deprived children whose parents refused to be bamboozled into buying breakfast cereals purely because you wanted to collect plastic figures or a set of 1957 Kellogg's Frosties 'Famous Frontier Guns'?

Collecting cereal packet gifts, and even cereal packets, is a popular hobby. Pioneered by the Americans, the idea of 'cereal box prizes' began with the collecting of box tops, which could be exchanged in store for prizes. This began in the early 20th century. By the mid-1940s Kellogg's were putting badges into boxes of Pep cereal, and various other manufacturers quickly followed suit. However, mailing off for prizes by collecting packet tops was still popular.

With the advent of low-cost injection moulding, cheap plastic gifts at breakfast time proved to be an irresistible draw to youngsters and no object was more popular than the baking powder submarine. This simple little mass-produced giveaway even has its own Wikipedia page. Devised by two brothers called Harry and Benjamin Hirsch in 1953, they sold the idea to the Kellogg

Company in 1954 and, as the web page describes, the popularity of the gift was 'buoyed by the launch of the first American atomic submarine, USS *Nautilus*, commissioned in that year'. Over a million were produced in 1954. Later variations on the theme included frogmen.

My favourite cereal packet giveaway has to be the Nestlé Stardust meteorite cards that were issued a few years ago in Shreddies packets. Fine shavings from various heavenly bodies were sealed in credit-card-sized packets; the dust apparently came from NASA where machined waste from experiments is thrown out. I was captivated; kids must have loved them. A complete set of twenty is worth around £500.

THE HISTORY OF HALLMARKS

Hallmarking is one of the oldest forms of consumer protection in the world; the British system of regulation dates back some 700 years to the reign of King Edward I. Edward passed a statute requiring silver to be of sterling standard, the same as coinage, and so the system of stamping silver with a series of marks was instituted. Initially, the Wardens of the Goldsmiths' Guild in London were responsible for assaying and the leopard's head we associate with the London assay office was created. Hallmarking is still carried out at Goldsmiths' Hall today.

As demand expanded, provincial offices were opened, including Edinburgh in the 15th century. Their stamp was a three-turreted castle, to which was added a thistle in 1759; this in turn was replaced in 1975 with a rampant lion.

The Birmingham and Sheffield offices were instituted in 1773; Birmingham is marked with an anchor and Sheffield a crown (replaced in 1974 with a rosette). The Dublin office was instituted in the mid-17th century and used a harp surmounted by a crown. This was supplemented in 1731 with a separate figure of Hibernia.

Marks were also assayed by a number of provincial offices no longer in operation:

Chester (closed in 1962)
Mark: three wheat sheaves and a sword

Exeter (closed in 1883)
Marks: a crowned X or a three-turreted castle

Glasgow (closed in 1964)
Mark: combined tree, bird, bell and fish

Newcastle upon Tyne (closed in 1884)
Mark: three separated turrets

Norwich (closed by 1701)
Mark: a crowned lion passant and a crowned rosette

York (closed in 1856)
Marks: half leopard's head, half fleur-de-lys; later five lions passant on a cross

British silver is some of the most collectable in the world, in no small way due to the assurance of hallmarking. Typically a well-marked piece of silver will carry a maker's mark such as 'HB' for Hester Bateman (1708–1794), a lion passant for the silver standard, an assay office mark (such as a leopard's head for the London assay office) and a date letter from the year of assaying, which in Hester's case might be 'a' for 1776. For an excellent reference book of British hallmarks see *Bradbury's Book of Hallmarks*, the pocket edition.

> Many provincial Scottish and Irish silversmiths didn't use the main assay offices and instead chose to just simply mark their work with a maker's mark. Rarity has made this type of silver highly sought after.

HERITAGE LOTTERY

Most countries have an export licensing system in place to protect their cultural heritage. This exists to prevent objects deemed of historic and cultural importance being exported without proper consultation. In the UK the process aims to protect our heritage for future generations, although it does not necessarily prohibit objects or art from leaving the country.

The Art Fund is a charity which acts as a national focus and fundraising organisation to raise money on appeal for works of art that have export 'holds'. This can often involve saving valuable works of art, furniture and paintings from being lost to overseas buyers. For example, if a major work of art is purchased at auction and the new owner applies for an export licence, time is given for organisations such as museums to match the purchase price and save the item for the nation. There have been many notable successes, for instance involving Canova's 'Three Graces', which was 'export stopped' in 1994 and saved at a cost of £7.7 million. It would have otherwise gone to the Getty Museum.

The Art Fund's first success was the 'The Rokeby Venus' by Diego Velázquez, acquired in 1906 at a cost of £45,000. All objects and works considered are examined under certain criteria, full details of which can be found on the government's cultural property advice website: www.culturalpropertyadvice.gov.uk

TEN A PENNY

Preserving tradition has become a nice
hobby, like stamp collecting
—Mason Cooley

Traditionally, it was every schoolboy philatelist's dream, the elusive stamp pictured at the top of the page in most albums – the Penny Black. The general perception, and one that still persists, is that it's the most valuable stamp you can own, but this little piece of important history is far more affordable than you might imagine.

The Penny Black was the result of a revolutionary idea to reform the antiquated and expensive British postal service, which was based on distance and weight. A low uniform rate seemed sensible and Rowland Hill's proposal of 1837 in his pamphlet *Post Office Reform; Its Importance and Practicability* resulted in a campaign backed by many businessmen, MPs and the public to introduce a fair and affordable system. It took over two years to be ratified by parliament but became law in 1839.

A competition was held for pre-paid postage designs, with some 2,600 entries received, ranging from printed envelopes to various forms of stamps, but it was the design for the 'adhesive labels' bearing Queen Victoria's head that won. The use of security measures such as 'white-line' machine engraving and lettering on the corners to indicate the position on the printed sheets helped to combat faking. Initially, it was proposed to charge 4d but this was later revised to 1d and on 1 April 1840 the first proof impressions were printed. On 1 May the 'labels' were put on sale in London ready for posting on the 6th. Six hundred thousand left the presses every day and some 68 million Penny Blacks were printed in under a year; a 2d Blue was also issued, which is much rarer than the Penny Black.

Initially Penny Blacks were cancelled with a red Maltese cross but it was soon discovered that this could be removed and as a result the printing ink was changed to a red-brown, to be cancelled with a black Maltese cross; this is the stamp we now refer to as the Penny Red. The introduction of the penny post was a massive and instant success, one that changed the world and instigated the start of stamp collecting as a pastime.

Penny Blacks vary in value enormously, depending on several important factors. Firstly, condition: mint stamps are obviously more valuable. Heavy cancellations can obliterate the stamp. Penny Blacks are not perforated and had to be cut with scissors by the postmaster; if the design is clipped the value is also affected. A well-centred stamp with clear, straight margins is the most desirable.

The plate from which the stamp was printed is also important. Each steel printing plate had 240 engraved stamps (adding up to a value of £1), and each had its own peculiar idiosyncrasies and characteristics. Determining which plate a stamp hails from is a specialist job but out of the eleven plates used, number eleven is the rarest as only 168,000 stamps were printed from that particular plate, as opposed to plate six with a total of 9,095,040. The fact is, a used Penny Black in poor condition from a high-production plate can cost as little as £30–40. A well-cut mint example from a low production plate can cost several thousand.

I have one Penny Black and I have it for one reason: it's a 19th-century fake and probably worth a good £50 for that reason alone.

The legendary Penny Black

THE ANTIQUES MAGPIE

OOH-ERR MISSUS

If there's one thing the British are good at, it's saucy seaside humour. Crude and often inappropriate seaside postcards seem to have become part of British culture. Their smutty jokes and double entendres, garish colours and comically executed characters are sure to raise a spontaneous snigger despite their sexist themes and stereotypes.

The most famous artist of the genre was Donald McGill. Born into a religious family in 1875, he sold his first design in 1905 to Asher's Pictorial Postcards. He was paid six shillings and it went on to sell over 2 million copies; by the 1930s, the industry had become colossal and McGill had produced over 12,000 designs; some estimates put his sales at 200–300 million but no one can be certain. At first, his cards had a comic patriotic theme but this progressed on to the more saucy variety and his fat-bottomed ladies and rosy-cheeked vicars are a trademark. One of his most famous cards, 'Do you like Kipling?', sold over 6 million alone, but it was 'It Girl' and 'Hard Rock' that were catapulted to mythical status when they were banned in 1953; police in Cleethorpes raided local shops and McGill was charged under the 1857 obscene publications act. He pleaded guilty and was fined but the industry went into decline as a result and although it bounced back a little in the 1960s, tastes eventually changed. However, McGill's cards are very popular among collectors and values range between £1 and £20 on average.

McGill was never paid any royalties and died in 1962 leaving an estate of just £735 – a sad epitaph for a man who made so many people laugh.

"Do you like Kipling?"
"I don't know, you naughty boy,
I've never kippled!"

One of Donald McGill's most popular postcards

VANITAS

The collector is an artist in his own way,
by the way he puts things together. You can
read a person's soul from their collection
—Ayers Tarantino

Have you ever stopped to wonder on the futility of life, the inevitability of it all, death? Well hopefully it's not something that preoccupies your thoughts too much, although for our ancestors it was a subject of great importance and much conjecture. Death was closer at hand in the medieval period and a far greater day-to-day reality than it is now. The theme was portrayed in art as *vanitas*, a Latin term that literally translates as 'vanity'. However, vanity had a different meaning than it does today and was more closely associated with the transient nature of life, the futility of earthly pleasures and the certainty of an appointment with the grim reaper.

The manifestation of vanitas in art was particularly fashionable in still-life paintings and sculpture, with motifs such as skulls, animal skeletons, rotting fruit, the hourglass and other more subtle variations being commonplace. Portraiture also utilised symbolic references and it was not unheard of for a sitter to be portrayed with a hand placed on a skull. The style was particularly prevalent in Low Countries art of the 16th and 17th centuries. 'Still Life: An Allegory of the Vanities of Human Life' by Harmen Steenwyck, painted c.1640, is an excellent example of a Dutch vanitas painting. Sculptural examples include carved ivory heads or skulls, often featured with half-intact, half-rotted faces with worms or snakes coiling from the eye sockets – a stark reminder of what death has in store. These objects are highly desirable among collectors, with most residing in museums. The Wellcome Collection in London and the British Museum have a number of excellent examples.

Similar to the theme of vanitas is the idea of a *memento mori*, an object or piece of art also made to signify the inevitability of death and the futility of earthly pleasures and achievement. *Memento mori* is Latin for 'remember you will die' or 'reminder of death' and just as vanitas-related items are highly collectable, so too are the macabre but compelling objects that fall into this genre. In collecting terms the type of artefacts that are highly sought after include snuff boxes, vesta cases (matchboxes) and vinaigrettes (for holding sweet-smelling oils) in the form of skulls and coffins; enamelled rings decorated with skulls and bones; and mourning rings imbued with symbolism.

Current fashion has seen a big resurgence in vanitas themes, fuelled in no small part by artists and designers such as Damien Hirst and Alexander McQueen; our high streets are filled with skull-themed merchandise and decorative objects – but few of us probably draw the same associations as a population reeling from the latest bout of the Black Death.

Nothing to do with chocolate, the term 'Kit-Cat' originates from the owner of a 'pye' shop: Christopher ('Kit') Catling. The famous Whig Kit-Cat Club founded by Sir Godfrey Kneller was named after him. Kneller also commissioned a series of portraits of the members (1702–17), which were executed on a standard-size canvas measuring 36 × 28in. This also became known as a Kit-Cat and, strictly speaking, portrayed the head, shoulders and one hand of the sitter.

LONDON BRIDGE IS FALLING DOWN

London's bridges have had a central role in the city's history. The relics of these old crossing points are remarkably fashionable with collectors. The iconic medieval bridge crowded with buildings was demolished in 1831; its 600-year-old structure was impeding shipping and it was no longer able to accommodate the volume of traffic crossing the Thames. Its demolition was a monumental task and like many great landmarks it was not uncommon for souvenirs to be fashioned from the fabric. Due to the anaerobic mud of the Thames, the 12th-century wooden piles were still solid and intact when removed, and some of the most commonly found souvenirs (although not abundant) are small wooden boxes fashioned from the piles.

The replacement granite bridge, designed by John Rennie, gave sterling service but by the 1960s had sunk some eight inches. Another new bridge was inevitable and in 1968 the old one was sold to Robert P. McCulloch, a wealthy American oil magnate. He shipped the granite elements all the way to Arizona via the Panama Canal, where it was re-erected – although there is a popular story that he thought he was buying that great symbol of London, Tower Bridge! Desk weights and other small souvenirs made from the granite can sometimes be found.

On a similar theme, during the Second World War, the Houses of Parliament were hit by Luftwaffe bombs. Stone from the damage was fashioned into bookends, desk weights, biscuit barrels and tobacco jars, each mounted with a metal plaque and sold in aid of the Red Cross. These are much sought after and have risen dramatically in price in recent years; it's not uncommon for a pair of bookends to achieve in the region of £200.

Souvenirs often rely on a strong association with famous or historical personalities and Nelson is always a great draw. His flagship, HMS *Foudroyant* was saved from a German scrapyard by public outcry and bought privately by a Victorian entrepreneur by the name of Joseph Wheatly Cobb; it then sailed around the coast as a tourist attraction. Unfortunately, in 1897, the ship foundered in a bad storm and was wrecked on Blackpool beach. She was sold for £200 but a vast amount of flotsam was used from the wreck to make all manner of items ranging from furniture to small trinkets. Similarly, given the many refits that HMS *Victory* has undergone, it's not uncommon to find souvenir plaques and objects made from the copper sheathing of the hull, and also wooden objects. Such items are usually mounted with small metal plaques. If you thought recycling was something new, think again!

LOST LEONARDO

A man paints with his brains and not with his hands
—Michelangelo

It was the art world sensation of 2011: the discovery of a long-lost work by Leonardo da Vinci. Painted for Louis XII of France between 1506 and 1513, the picture of Christ known as '*Salvator Mundi*' (Saviour of the World) was also catalogued as part of the collection of Charles I of England. It was recorded as being sold in 1763 and later acquired in 1900 by Frederick Cook, a British art collector. By this time its attribution to Leonardo had been lost, its identity hidden under layers of poor restoration and dirt. Cook sold it in 1958 for £45.

Its re-emergence in 2005 led to a long and painstaking restoration and consultation. Now owned by an American consortium and Robert Simon, the New York art dealer and Da Vinci expert, initial interpretations were extremely cautious, swaying towards it having been painted by a follower of the great Renaissance painter. However, as the layers were stripped away, the realisation began to dawn on Simon and his restorer, Dianne Dwyer Modestini, that this could be the first Leonardo to be discovered in over 100 years. Several clues made the attribution a possibility, including alterations typical of Leonardo's work, known as 'pentimento'; the artist had altered the position of Christ's thumb.

Further consultation with the world's top experts eventually compounded the importance of the discovery and after seven years of painstaking restoration and research Leonardo's lost image of Christ was put on show at the National Gallery's groundbreaking 2011/12 exhibition 'Leonardo da Vinci: Painter at the Court of Milan'. It is thought to be worth in excess of £100 million.

> Tempera is one of the oldest forms of paint known; it was used in ancient Egypt and can be found on mummy sarcophagi. Up until c.1500 it was the most popular medium for European panel painting in the medieval period. Formed from ground pigment mixed with a binder such as honey, glue or egg yolk, it is known for being resilient. All of Michelangelo's surviving works on panel are painted in egg tempera.

1933 PENNY

On countless occasions over the years I have been handed large bags and boxes of copper coinage; the owners have then folded their arms and asked, 'Do you think there's a 1933 penny in there?' My standard reply is a simple 'no', usually without even taking the trouble to look. If this sounds flippant, perhaps a little explanation is needed.

The 1933 penny has acquired a folkloric, legendary status among coin collectors and the public. In 1933, the banks had huge stocks of pennies, making it unnecessary to strike any more that year. However, the tradition of putting coins under the foundations of new buildings meant that at least three were struck expressly for that purpose. Unfortunately, accurate records were not kept of how many were actually created. It's thought perhaps six or seven at most were struck, including 'record' examples for the British Museum and Royal Mint. But it became part of the public perception that it might be possible to find one in your change. The likelihood of this happening is even smaller than winning the lottery.

In 1970, an example was stolen from the foundation of the Church of St Cross, Middleton, near Leeds, prompting another to be removed for safety. In 2009 a specimen was sold privately for £80,000. If a further 1933 penny were to be offered for sale, that price would no doubt be surpassed. There have been several attempts to circulate fakes in the marketplace. One turned up on eBay recently but was mysteriously withdrawn.

JAPANESE DRESS SENSE

Originating in 17th-century Japan, *netsuke* – pronounced 'net-ski' – are often intricately carved tiny works of art fashioned from an amazing variety of materials, including elephant ivory, marine ivory, coral, bone, wood, amber, fossilised wood and Tagua nut. They are highly esteemed among collectors and connoisseurs and like many Japanese objects have an allure and sense of ritual not commonly found in European artefacts, being both tactile and functional.

Traditional Japanese robes had no pockets, so in order for men to be able to carry personal items they used small pouches or woven baskets. The most valued of these containers are called *inrō*. Often lacquered, these sectional boxes (each with a different name) are threaded with cords. In order to keep the sections together they utilised a netsuke and an *ojime*, a small carved bead that could be pulled tight on the cord. All three are collected, together or in their own right.

Of course, as with anything desirable and collectable, the demand for netsuke has led to the market being swamped by cheap copies heralding from China and other Eastern countries, often hand-carved but of poor artistic merit; others are made of plastics and resins and coloured to look old.

Netsuke are often signed; known, sought-after carvers can attract high values. The Bluette H. Kirchhoff collection sold by Bonham's in New York in 2009 had some wonderful examples, several achieving $50,000–60,000 each. In 2011, the Bonham's sale of the Harriet Szechenyi collection of Japanese works of art saw an 18th-century ivory netsuke of a *shishi* (Lion of Fo) sell for £265,250. In the same sale, a 19th-century inrō also made £250,250.

SWORDPLAY

The Japanese sword is a technological masterpiece and a work of art. There are several types of Japanese sword, each constructed from several component parts and historically varied in size and application. The most common lengths are the *katana*, *wakizashi* and *tantō*, the tantō being the shortest – more like a knife. The katana is the sword that we associate most with the samurai and was used from the 15th century onwards.

The construction of a Japanese blade is a highly

specialised and technical process, using a mixture of steels to produce shock-absorbent blades of differing profile and design. Even the point on a Japanese blade has various specialised forms and each face, facet, border and edge has a different name. Blades can be folded or 'welded' many thousands of time to produce distinctive patterns, some of which are attributable to particular sword makers. Other parts of the sword such as the *tsuba* (guard) and *fuchi kashira* (butt) are considered works of art in their own right and are collected as such.

The golden age of Japanese swordsmithing is considered to be from 987 to 1597. Examples from this period are known as *kotō* or 'old swords'. Over 100 swords are listed as National Treasures in Japan, one of them dating from the Kofun period of 250–538.

Blades by masters such as Masamune, c.1264–1343, widely considered to be Japan's greatest swordsmith, can no longer be removed from the country. A Masamune blade was given to American president Harry S. Truman after the Second World War. It can be seen in the Harry S. Truman Presidential Library and Museum in Independence, Missouri. Some modern Japanese sword makers are considered 'living National Treasures' and a prize in Masamune's name is awarded at the National Japanese Sword-making Competition.

The fact that such rare swords are unlikely to come up for sale, and that those known examples cannot leave Japan, makes valuing difficult. However, a 13th-century Kamakura from the Compton Collection of Japanese Swords was sold in New York by Christie's in 1992 for $418,000. The sale made $8 million on the first day.

Japanese sword parts

Saya – scabbard

Sageo – belt cord

Fuchi kashira – the fitting on the butt or pommel

Nakago – the tang inside the *tsuka* where the sword is
likely to be signed

Tsuka – the hilt or grip held in position with a bamboo
peg, which passes through a hole in the tang

Same – the ray-skin grip that covers the tsuka

Ito – the cord that is woven around the ray skin

Menuki – the charms that are woven under the ito

Mekugi – the bamboo pin that holds the tsuka in
position

Tsuba – the cut guard

Habaki – a square brass or iron collar below the tsuba
that holds it in place

Hamon – the 'wave' along the edge of blade caused by
tempering

Hada – the grain of the blade

Hi – the blood groove

Yaiba – the cutting edge

Kissaki – the tip

CLOISONNÉ OR CHAMPLEVÉ?

Generally associated with being an oriental art form, the
production of enamelled metal wares has been practised
by the Chinese and Japanese for centuries. *Cloisonné* and
champlevé are two processes that are commonly mixed
up. The difference between them is a technicality that

produces a distinctly different effect. Champlevé, as used by the Romans, entails cutting back the surface of a relatively thick metal object and filling the voids with fired enamel paste. It is usually executed on bronze or brass. Cloisonné involves sticking small wires or *cloisonnes* to the surface of a metal object and firing the glass paste within them. Copper is the usual choice but due to its softness, cloisonné items are often dented and damaged. Cloisonné is a particularly painstaking process. Both require various stages of polishing after firing.

CHINESE WHISPERS

Any 18th-century aristocrat with taste would have kept up with the Joneses by ordering his porcelain from China. It was de rigueur to have entire armorial services specially commissioned; in order to do this a design of the family arms would be drawn up and sent with an agent all the way to Jingdezhen in China. Understandably, this was quite a long process given the distances and work involved. Imagine then, after expectantly waiting a couple of years for your 400-piece service to arrive, you finally take delivery of it only to find every piece incorrectly decorated: all the peripheral instructions denoting the colour of the family arms, such as 'paint this red, paint this blue' – and even spelling mistakes – have all been faithfully transferred to the finished product. Although not common, a number of such occurrences have been documented. One famous service was annotated with 'in blue and white'. Such wonderful literal mistakes and anomalies are the kind of idiosyncrasies that fire collectors.

AUSTERITY MEASURES

Austerity might be a popular watchword in our recession-hit times but just spare a thought for consumers during the Second World War. In order to spare precious resources, rationing extended far beyond just food. Clothing was made from recycled specially printed flour sacks, ceramic production was limited to plain utilitarian designs and furniture was restricted to around 20 standardised models, decided by a committee of eminent designers headed by Gordon Russell.

This 'Utility' system was introduced in 1941 and continued until 1953. The symbol used to mark the pieces is considered a classic piece of graphic design.

The Utility mark; 'CC41' represents
'controlled commodity' and the date, 1941

Interest among collectors in these once-disregarded, functional Utility designs has increased dramatically over the years, so it's worth taking a look underneath Granny's furniture to see if you can spot the mark.

GNOME ALONE

It's easy to poke fun at people who populate their front gardens with garishly painted reconstituted 'little folk'. Garden gnomes tend to attract rather bad press on the whole and are oft maligned as kitsch concrete accessories unworthy of anywhere other than the suburban gardens where they crowd around ponds and nestle in rockeries. However, gnomes have far more aristocratic origins. Similar creatures first started appearing in the early 17th century. *Gobbi* (Italian for dwarf) can be seen in the engravings of Jacques Callot, the baroque print-maker, and by the 18th century carved stone grotesque dwarf-like creatures had started to appear in grand gardens on the Continent.

Early gnomes of the form in which we know them were not strictly intended for the garden, and it seems likely that a transition period for mantelpiece 'little folk', turned out en masse in the porcelain factories of Thuringia, happened sometime in the early 19th century. The factory of Alfred Baehr and Johann Maresch seems to have the strongest claim for producing the first ceramic outdoor gnomes in the early 1840s, and as the industry expanded the idea of larger-scale pottery gnomes became increasingly popular. Trade catalogues of the mid- to late 19th century show wonderful examples of gnomes in every guise from gun-toting hunters to their more traditional role as miners.

Credited as the father of British 'gnomery' was Sir Charles Isham (1819–1903). He installed a spectacular alpine rockery at his home, Lamport Hall in

Northamptonshire, in 1847 and populated it with gnomes. He was a spiritualist and was apparently convinced of the existence of fairies. His garden became famous for the gnomes and was featured in many publications such as *Country Life* and *Strand Magazine*. The Victorians wholeheartedly accepted gnomes into their gardens without there being any suggestion of bad taste. Sadly, only one of the original gnomes survives from Sir Charles' rockery; he's affectionately known as 'Lampy' and can be seen at Lamport Hall. Apparently, he is insured for £1 million.

The decline of the gnome is in no small part due to the anti-German sentiment of the First World War. Most German goods were boycotted and gnomes were one of the casualties. The high-quality German terracotta gnomes were replaced in the inter-war period by concrete examples and the social status of the gnome declined into the cheap and chirpy garden ornaments we associate so strongly with 'bad taste'. Their image hasn't been helped over the years by the rash of plastic and composite versions baring their bottoms and holding mobile phones. Yet, all is not lost. Gnome appreciation varies in style; there are those that love them for their kitsch appeal and there are those who take them very seriously. Old gnomes are very collectable. I recently filmed a wonderful 1920s terra-cotta pixie on a giant toadstool on the *Antiques Roadshow*; I would have happily put it in my garden – had I had £600 to spare! Rare Johann Maresch examples can make in excess of £2,000.

> *Putti* are a common theme in art history.
> These pink plump male infants are a secular
> version of cherubim, which originate from the
> Hebrew Bible and are an order of angel in later
> Christian doctrines. Putti (an Italian term) do
> not necessarily have wings, and are not to be
> confused with Cupid, who does have wings
> and is often portrayed later in art history in
> multiples known as *amorini*. Context is important
> – hopefully the next time an argument breaks
> out in a spectacular Continental cathedral this
> will quickly clear up any misunderstandings.

FAKE DINOSAURS

*It isn't easy to become a fossil. Only about one bone in a
billion, it is thought, becomes fossilised. If that is so, it
means that the complete fossil legacy of all the Americans
alive today – that's 270 million people with 206 bones
each – will only be about 50 bones, one-quarter of
a complete skeleton. That's not to say, of course, that
any of these bones will ever actually be found.*
—Bill Bryson

The collecting of fossils and natural history specimens
has seen a complete renaissance in recent years. Fossil and
mineral sales have rocketed and large sales conventions
are particularly popular, especially in America. With such
a ready market, the trade in fake fossils has multiplied

enormously and is mainly supplied by the Chinese, who seem to have an amazing aptitude for tapping into such veins.

One of the biggest scandals to emerge was the announcement in 1999, in *National Geographic* magazine, of a 'missing link', a hitherto unknown fossil bird. It was named 'Archaeoraptor' and attracted worldwide media attention. Unfortunately, after further scientific investigation, it turned out to be a very clever composite fake, made out of several different fossils including the head and body of an actual fossilised bird. The incident highlighted the problems facing collectors and museums in a market where such potential discoveries can be worth hundreds of thousands of pounds.

Despite a blanket ban on exporting fossils from China, with stiff penalties for offenders, there are a myriad of fakes on the market and the forgers have become increasingly sophisticated. Mixing real specimens with false elements is rife and even using bones and skulls from real creatures such as chickens and setting them into man-made matrixes, adding different teeth and so forth, is common. A quick search on eBay with the words 'fossil teeth' immediately revealed a selection of real Mosasaur teeth set in fake jawbone-style matrixes. Most of these herald from North Africa.

The most expensive fossil ever discovered is the Tyrannosaurus Rex specimen found in 1990 by palaeontologist Sue Hendrickson. It was sold in 1997 for £4 million. However, if you're chasing a few specimens yourself it's important to remember the old adage, 'if it looks too good to be true then it probably is'.

NAME CHECK

A quick flick through an auction catalogue will no doubt throw up lots of names and words that you don't tend to come across in everyday life, many of which, if investigated, prove to have surprising and fascinating etymologies. A common example you'll encounter in the world of antiques is the **loo table**. Nothing to do with toilets, the name derives from the game of lanterloo, a card game that originated in the 17th century and became one of the most popular games in England, much favoured by the 'rich and idle'. Most examples you'll see will have an oval or circular top, which has a mechanism to tip it over for easier storage; such tables generally date from the 19th century.

The **Pembroke table** is a small drop-leaf side table or 'occasional' table that apparently owes its name to Henry Herbert, the 9th Earl of Pembroke (1693–1751). He was a notable collector and amateur architect. The two flaps can be raised and supported on brackets called 'elbows' and most Pembroke tables have a drawer at one end, or perhaps both. It's a style of table that remained popular through the 19th and into the early 20th century.

The **Wellington chest** is generally accepted as a tall narrow chest of usually eight to twelve drawers, with a hinged vertical side flap that locks all the drawers in place. A drop-flap secretaire for writing is sometimes incorporated. It takes its name from Sir Arthur Wellesley (1769–1852), the 1st Duke of Wellington, and its design originated from 'campaign furniture', or furniture that was specifically designed for travelling – not just for military officers as the name suggests.

The **Sutherland table** is a small drop-leaf table with a narrow top that makes it easy to store. It is believed to have been named after Harriet, Duchess of Sutherland (1806–1868) and was used for tea or breakfast. Most models you'll see are 19th century but the style continued through the Edwardian period.

The **cricket table** draws some obvious associations by virtue of its name. These three-legged tables with circular tops originated in the 17th century and were initially quite fine in form, sometimes with turned elements, but are more often found in rougher versions with a lower shelf – a type popular in taverns (on uneven floors, three legs find their feet far better than four). Although an early form of the game of cricket existed in this period it's unlikely that the name has anything to do with the game; it's far more likely that the word is a corruption of the word 'cracket' – a type of three-legged stool that was named in the early 17th century. The supposition that the three legs are associated with the three stumps is rather fanciful.

The **Davenport** is a small, relatively portable desk with an inclined overhanging 'lift-up' writing surface, usually flanked by two decorative supports. Some have a central cupboard and drawers on either side. Rolls-Royce versions sometimes have spring-operated rise and fall stationery compartments in the top. The name apparently derives from a Captain Davenport who ordered the first model in the late 18th century from the prestigious Gillows of Lancaster.

The **Canterbury** is a small piece of furniture with divisions in the top, rather like a magazine rack (and often used for that purpose today), usually with a small frieze drawer and raised up on short legs and casters. It was originally designed for sheet music and by all accounts acquired its name from an Archbishop of Canterbury who ordered one in the late 18th century.

Fancy cupboards, particularly boulle- and marble-topped examples, are often catalogued as '**credenzas**'. The word is actually Italian for cupboard.

Armoire is a word generally used for large cupboards or wardrobes but should generally apply to French and Continental examples. The origin is quite simply that they were used for storing armour; later on, particularly in the 18th and 19th centuries, they were produced in France with narrow doors and slender compartments in the side for keeping guns.

The **Windsor** chair is a well-known style, although there are many design variations. Regional versions of stick-back or comb-back chairs are well documented but the actual origin or age of the Windsor is not known. As a generic variation on a local type of chair, it could have developed from the 16th century onwards from the tradition of forest wood-turning. The characteristic steam-bent back that we associate with the chair was first made in the Berkshire town of Windsor in the early 18th century and it's thought that this is the most likely origin for the name.

MARC ALLUM FECIT, 2013

Sometimes found on sculpture, prints and other objects, the Latin word *fecit* means 'made' or 'did' and is sometimes written as '*fec.*', '*fect.*', or just plain '*f.*'.

'John Smith *fecit*, 1769' basically means 'John Smith made me [the item] in 1769'.

MADE TO KILL

Antique arms and armour hold a strange fascination for collectors. Some weapons are utilitarian and made with a sole purpose; some are a tour de force of the craftsman's art and made for presentation purposes; others are imbued with history from famous owners. Whatever the reason for collecting, there is an undeniable romance attached to some of these artefacts, an attraction vested in another age for weapons infused with heroic symbolism, where chivalry and etiquette dictated battlefield practices, the demise of empires and the rise of others. It's a man thing.

Some of the most impressive objects sold in recent years have had impeccable pedigrees. In 2007 General Ulysses S. Grant's Civil War presentation sword sold at Heritage Auction Galleries in Dallas for $1.673 million. A magnificent pair of pistols by Nicolas-Noël Boutet, once owned by Simon Bolivar, the first president of Venezuela, was sold in New York by Christie's in 2004 for $1.74 million; another pair of pistols owned by President George Washington was sold in New York by Christie's in 2002 for $1.96 million. In 2008 a Mughal dagger owned by Shah Jahan, the emperor who built the Taj Mahal, was sold by Bonham's in London for £1.7 million. But the most expensive antique weapon ever to be sold was in 2007 when the last remaining sword belonging to Napoleon and still in private hands was put up for auction in Fontainebleau. Believed to have been used in battle by him, it raised a staggering €4.8 million (£3.3 million).

FLAG DAY

It's the stuff of legend. The 1876 battle of Little Bighorn in Montana where George Armstrong Custer made his last stand against the Lakota Sioux and Cheyenne warriors; he was killed along with over 200 of his troopers on that fateful day. Custer's reputation is debatable but the outcome was not. His soldiers were carrying five flags known as 'guidon' at the battle. The pennant-shaped standards were lost, all except one, which was found under the body of Corporal John Foley three days after the slaughter. A Sergeant Ferdinand Culbertson, part of the burial party, retrieved the flag and it was thence known as the 'Culbertson guidon'. It was purchased by the Detroit Institute of Arts in 1895 for $54. It was sold by Sotheby's in New York in December 2010 for the equivalent of £1.4 million.

CLEAN ME

It's an all-too-common problem: people love to clean things but cleaning can do untold damage to antique items and can cause the value to plummet. Bronzes are a favourite for the 'Brasso' treatment and I've seen many a good object shined to within an inch of its life by an unsuspecting, well-meaning owner. Bronze patination is part of the sculptural and artistic integrity of an object and also employed to give cast-bronze objects a uniformity of colour that might cover some imperfections and repairs within the casting process. Luckily, the finishes can be restored – at a price. On the whole, it's always sensible to take the advice of a professional when it comes to cleaning or restoration. Within acceptable economic limits, it's possible to restore most things.

Paintings need expert help, although there are some basic tasks you can take on at home, such as light cleaning to remove nicotine, for instance. Professional restorers use saliva on a cotton swab; it's a painstaking process but one that you can attempt if you have the patience. The enzymes in saliva are a good cleaning agent. A light polish using museum-grade restorer's wax is also acceptable, and general maintenance of old oil paintings can include making sure that the canvas is taut by ensuring that the stretcher keys (wooden wedges) are in place and that the picture is well-hung, away from smoky hearths and red-hot radiators!

With coins it is more a case of conserving than actually restoring. The last thing you should do is clean a coin. Any abrasion on the surface can cause untold damage so no commercial products should be employed. Warm water with a mild detergent is fine but pat dry and do not rub the surfaces. A gentle application of museum wax afterwards will help protect further.

Furniture is wonderfully resilient and a good restorer can work wonders with even the worst-looking casualties. DIY is mainly limited to waxing and general common-sense maintenance but don't be worried about replacing the odd piece of popped veneer: central heating plays havoc with the old rabbit-skin glue!

The problem is that most of us live with our antiques on a day-to-day basis. Dogs lie all over the Persian carpets and we hoover them continually. Light falls on antique textiles and 18th-century chairs sit by the Aga monopolised by the cat. It's difficult if you are too precious; after all, we don't live in museums and there would be no enjoyment in living with such things if they could never be utilised. It's about finding a balance between appreciation and preservation: some of us call it shabby chic – it's a quintessentially British style that graces many an interiors magazine.

SOCIAL WORKER

Auctioneering is a strange profession. In many respects, auctioneers are little more than glorified second-hand salesmen; in others they are capable of scaling the pinnacles of the art world and revelling in the kudos of great discovery and financial reward. The pursuit of the valuable, rare and unusual is a constant motivator, the desire to divine the next £1 million Chinese vase or a rare manuscript perhaps. However, the fact of the matter is that most auctioneers cut their teeth and gain their experience in the general world of chattels, where the nitty-gritty of acquiring goods for sale is most likely based on the demise of their fellow human beings. I've often said that auctioneering is as much about dealing with death as dealing with antiques, and that 50 per cent of the remit is based on the ability to work sensitively with bereavement or other difficult situations such as divorce or a client moving into a retirement home.

It's a job that is more than the sum of all its parts

because if you are serious about doing it properly it has more facets than a brilliant cut diamond. It allows you to indulge your interests, your skill and knowledge, to meet amazing people, talk with passionate collectors and visit wonderful houses and institutions.

Among the many poignant situations you are likely to encounter are the shocking stories of reclusive characters that survived on chocolate bars and milk and lived in rat-infested rubbish dumps with no electricity and only one cold tap. It's about stepping over the stains on the floor where they lay for many weeks before they were even missed.

It's a job that tests your emotional resilience and your patience; it reveals the avaricious side of human nature and the kinder side too. It's a profession that takes you through every social class because death and collecting cross all divides.

Hopefully, when you have done your job as the social worker, there is a little bit of energy left to enjoy the fruits of your labours: the opportunity to see things find new homes with other passionate collectors, to effectively deal with an estate that may well have ended up in a skip, and to go home at the end of the day without taking too many of other people's trials and tribulations back with you. I've always maintained that auctioneering is not for the faint-hearted.

ACKNOWLEDGEMENTS

You start to realise that things have gone seriously wrong when you find yourself dressing up in period costume. Re-enactment is often ridiculed by onlookers, who see the re-enactors as 'eccentrics'. But working with art and antiques is very much about dipping your toe into other epochs; dressing up can bring you closer to history and the other people who appreciate it. Wearing period costume doesn't necessarily mean you've lost the plot but it's an indicator that you've taken it to the next level of eccentricity.

I once threw a dinner party at a château I owned in France. It was themed along 18th-century lines, so I donned my outfit, popped on my powdered wig and delighted in entertaining the guests with a perfectly set table of period glass and ceramics, authentic punch and a Hogarthian menu that included pomegranate jellies that had trouble setting in the French summer heat. There was a point in the evening's proceedings, as the gilded sugared almonds shimmered in the candlelight, my head itched from the man-made fibres of the wig and I poured another glass of Madeira, that I did wonder about my sanity – but not for long.

Living close to history has always been part of my life: the wonderful houses I've owned, the varied collections I've amassed, the access that my work has given me and the privilege of meeting wonderful people, visiting superlative collections and having the opportunity to put the words on to paper for a book like this.

My long-suffering wife Lisa and my daughter Tallulah have demonstrated remarkable patience over the years and have been a great support as I've mused over the content of this book. Luckily Lisa shares many of my loves when it comes to objects and we agree on most things regarding style and art.

Icon have been wonderful; they are without doubt the most supportive publishers I have ever worked with and I would like to thank everybody involved with this book for their patience and trust in giving me carte blanche to write about a subject that they have never tackled before; this also allowed me to include a considerable amount of personal material. I would also like to thank Penny Britain for effecting an introduction to this wonderful publishing house and many of my other colleagues on the *Roadshow* for their help and input, including Geoffrey Munn, Rupert Maas, Philip Mould, Paul Atterbury, Hilary Kay and Lars Tharp. Thank you also to Simon Shaw, my series editor at the BBC for his continued support over the years.

Lastly, to history itself, the omnipotent generator that spins the intangible hands of that most esoteric subject – time; or is it the other way around? Without it where would I be, where would we be? Thank you.

APPENDIX I
AT A GLANCE BRITISH AND
FRENCH MONARCHS

British
Tudor
Henry VII	1485–1509
Henry VIII	1509–1547
Edward VI	1547–1553
Mary I	1553–1558
Elizabeth I	1558–1603

Stuart
James I (VI of Scotland)	1603–1625
Charles I	1625–1649
(Commonwealth)	1649–1660
Charles II	1660–1685
James II (VII of Scotland)	1685–1688
William III	1689–1702
Mary II	1689–1694
Anne	1702–1714

Hanover
George I	1714–1727
George II	1727–1760
George III	1760–1820
(Regency)	1811–1820
George IV	1820–1830

William IV	1830–1837
Victoria	1837–1901
Edward VI	1901–1910

Windsor

George V	1910–1936
Edward VIII	1936
George VI	1936–1952
Elizabeth II	1952–

French
Bourbon Dynasty

Henry IV	1539–1610
Louis XIII	1610–1643
Louis XIV	1643–1715
Louis XV	1715–1774
Louis XVI	1774–1792

First Republic

| National Convention | 1792–1795 |
| Directoire | 1795–1799 |

First Empire

Napoleon I	1804–1814
Louis XVIII (King)	1814–1815
Napoleon I	1815

Bourbons

| Louis XVIII | 1814–1824 |
| Charles X | 1824–1830 |

Orléans
Louis Philippe   1830–1848

Second Republic
Louis-Eugène Cavaignac   1848
Louis Napoleon   1848–1852
(Louis) Napoleon III   1852–1870

Third Republic
(Presidents)   1870–1906

APPENDIX II
A BRIEF GUIDE TO PERIODS AND STYLES

Where dates are given in bold, they typically refer to the period of rule of the monarch after whom the style is known, or a comparable historical backdrop. They are supplied to give a rough sense of timings. Attempting to pin down the exact dates when a style occurred would in most cases be an impossible task.

Gothic
European style from the 12th to the 16th century. Most work was of religious influence including pointed arches, stained-glass windows, quatrefoils and galleries.

Tudor
Spanning the first half of the 16th century, the Tudor period heralded the start of more perpendicular architecture, heavy linen-fold carving and vaulted ceilings.

Elizabethan (1558–1603)
Characterised by a tendency for ornamentation concocted from Gothic, Flemish and Italian Renaissance styles, many major manor houses were built in this period.

Jacobean (1603–1688)
Slightly more refined in style than Elizabethan but

retaining many of its characteristics. Carved oak and classical shapes with arcades and pilasters were strong features.

Baroque
Of 17th-century Italian origin, this style is associated with elaborate ornamentation – typical motifs include cornucopia – and bold curvaceous forms.

Cromwellian (1649–1660)
The Puritan style often referred to as 'Commonwealth', with plain forms and little ornamentation other than woodturning.

Carolean or Restoration (1660–1685)
The return of Charles II from exile in 1660 brought a new appreciation of Continental styles. English taste was revolutionised in many ways through simpler design and symmetry and the introduction of smaller purpose-made pieces of furniture such as dressing tables and bureaux.

William and Mary (1689–1702)
A strong Dutch influence brought by William of Orange from Holland promoted a fashion for heavy furniture with bold carving and oriental lacquer work.

Queen Anne (1702–1714)
Extending into the 1720s, the Queen Anne style promoted well-proportioned furniture mainly veneered in walnut with smooth, uncarved surfaces and 'cabriole' legs.

THE ANTIQUES MAGPIE

Palladian

A school of architecture inspired by the 16th-century Italian Palladio, whose designs were in turn inspired by ancient Rome. The Palladian style was popularised in England in the 18th century in the Neoclassical movement, by Robert Adam in particular.

Georgian (1714–1830)

A period that covers the reigns of George I–George IV. Georgian, in contrast to the baroque style, is more restrained and influenced by the Palladian and classical styles; rooms were painted in pale colours and dressed with elegant furniture.

Rococo (c.1730–1760)

Associated with the reign of Louis XV of France and seen as an evolutionary progression of the baroque style; its fluid, scrolling lines with c-scrolls, cartouches, birds, rocaille (rockwork) and shells are common motifs. Furniture was constructed to be beautiful and comfortable, with scrolling cabriole legs.

Neoclassical

Louis XVI's accession was followed by a reaction against Rococo extravagances; styles became simplified and furniture assumed tapering legs with flat or low-relief anthemion and patera decorations. Typical motifs were arrows, musical instruments, urns, husks and swags.

Thomas Chippendale

Chippendale (1718–1779) was the foremost cabinet maker

of his day, whose book *The Cabinet Maker's Director* was widely used as a pattern book by furniture makers. The distinctive mid-18th-century look of Chippendale furniture is characterised by square outlines and fret carved decoration and often has an oriental flavour (known as 'Chinese Chippendale').

George Hepplewhite

Another cabinet maker, Hepplewhite (d.1786), gives his name to a more restrained, lighter style than Chippendale with graceful lines and delicate motifs such as festoons and feathers.

Robert Adam

Adam (1728–1792) was an architect and designer in the Neoclassical style. These designs are characterised by delicate and graceful lines.

Thomas Sheraton

Sheraton (1751–1806) was a Neoclassical furniture designer. This is a style with an emphasis on straight vertical lines.

Directoire

Following the execution of Louis XVI in 1793, there was a move away from the over-ornamentation of the style of the French kings to a more restrained style. The furniture is typically painted rather than veneered.

Regency (1800–1830)

Fine quality furniture with plain lines typically veneered

in mahogany or rosewood and often with ormolu mounts. Popular motifs include Egyptian and nautical decoration, especially in the period following the Napoleonic wars.

Empire (1804–1815)
Representing Napoleon's empire and the glorification of his military campaigns with clean symmetrical lines, often with ormolu mounts. Typical motifs include urns, masks, imperial eagles, bees, laurel wreaths and trophies of war inspired by ancient Rome.

Biedermeier
Originating in Germany and Eastern Europe in the early 19th century and named after the German nickname for the bourgeoisie, its functional, middle-class furniture is simple in style and usually veneered in cherry and pale-coloured woods.

William IV (1830–1837)
A continuation of the Regency style.

Victorian (1837–1901)
In an age characterised by eclecticism, the furniture became more ornate but drew on many revivals of style; most were clever pastiches rather than exact copies. The Victorians invented modern consumerism with the advent of mass production.

Aesthetic movement
English artistic movement of the late 19th century based

on the theory of 'Art for Art's Sake'. Aubrey Beardsley and Oscar Wilde were closely associated with the movement.

Gothic Revival

A strong resurgence of interest in Gothic architecture in the late 18th and early 19th centuries was illustrated by Horace Walpole's redesign of his house, 'Strawberry Hill' in Twickenham, into a 'Gothick' castle, and spawned a whole new genre of Gothicism. Later buildings tended to be heavier and less whimsical in style, with notable public constructions being Augustus Pugin's Houses of Parliament (1836–65) and Gilbert Scott's St Pancras Station Hotel (1869–74).

Arts and Crafts

An English movement of the late 19th century, conceived as a reaction against mass production and advocating a return to traditional craftsmanship with no unnecessary ornamentation. William Morris and John Ruskin are regarded as being the founders of the movement.

Art Nouveau

Spanning from the late 19th century up until the First World War and popular all over Europe, styles were naturalistic, with asymmetric shapes highly decorated with tendrils of plants, flowers, and maidens with long, flowing hair.

Edwardian (1901–1910)

A watered-down reprisal of Neoclassical and Georgian styles with often inlaid furniture.

Art Deco

Named after *l'Exposition des Arts Décoratifs*, Paris, 1925, it is characterised by lively geometric patterns and clean, angular lines, in stark contrast with Art Nouveau.

Modernism

A dominant movement in 20th-century architecture with its main theory of 'form follows function' gaining momentum after the Second World War as a model for the rebuilding of European cities. Notable Modernists include Le Corbusier and Mies van der Rohe.

Pop Art

An influential cultural movement of the 1960s characterised by brightly coloured, often disposable objects and typified by the art of Andy Warhol and Roy Lichtenstein.

BIBLIOGRAPHY

General resources consulted
Oxford English Dictionary, Oxford University Press, online
    access, 2013
www.brainyquote.com (quotes)
www.goodreads.com (quotes)
www.todayinsci.com (quotes)
www.newguineaart.com (quotes)
www.wikipedia.com

Sources regarding specific entries
Websites
http://www.edinburghgeolsoc.org/edingeologist/z_27_06.html
    (Mythical Objects)
http://www.utexas.edu/tmm/npl/meteorites/tektites/tektite_info.
    html (Mythical Objects)
http://www.oldgardentools.co.uk/lawn-grooming (lawn boots)
http://www.hintsandthings.co.uk/games/collectors.htm
    (What's in a Name?)
http://cigarlabelgazette.com/articles/collectbands.html
    (What's in a Name?)
http://www.wondersandmarvels.com/2012/09/the-strange-
    journey-of-napoleons-penis.html (Napoleon's Penis)
http://www.buddhanet.net/deathtib.htm (Napoleon's Penis)
http://www.thesun.co.uk/sol/homepage/news/3263185/Albert-
    Einsteins-brain-sells-at-auction.html (Einstein's brain)
http://www.telegraph.co.uk/finance/currency/8655250/
    The-10-most-expensive-coins-in-the-world-in-pictures.
    html?image=3 (Coining it)
http://www.dailymail.co.uk/news/article-2099031/Rare-Double-
    Eagle-1933-coin-worth-7-6-MILLION-goes-UK-time.
    html (Coining it)

http://www.telegraph.co.uk/news/newstopics/howaboutthat/
    7856041/Worlds-largest-gold-coin-sold-for-2.7m.html
    (Coining it)

http://lunaticg.blogspot.co.uk/2011/02/most-valuable-british-
    coin-double.html (Coining it)

http://www.londoncrownglass.co.uk/London_Crown_Glass/
    History.html (Looking Glass)

http://www.cmog.org/ (Corning Museum) (Looking Glass)

http://www.britishmuseum.org/search_results.aspx?searchText=
    portland+vase&q=portland+vase (Looking Glass)

http://regencyredingote.wordpress.com/2011/01/07/alphabet-
    of-gems-the-language-of-stones-during-the-regency/
    (The Language of Jewellery)

http://www.vam.ac.uk/content/articles/h/jewellery-through-
    the-ages/ (The Language of Jewellery)

http://www.webring.org/l/rd?ring=hairworkwebring2;id=3;url=
    http%3A%2F%2Fsentimentaljewelry%2Eblogspot%2Eco
    %2Euk%2F2008%2F03%2Fmaking-silent-stones-
    speak%2Ehtml (The Language of Jewellery)

http://csmt.uchicago.edu/glossary2004/kitsch.htm (Tretchikoff
    – King of Kitsch?)

http://www.mirror.co.uk/news/world-news/chinese-girl-vladimir-
    tretchikoff-sells-1775039 (Tretchikoff – King of Kitsch?)

http://www.bloomberg.com/news/2013-01-30/durer-rhinoceros-
    fetches-record-866-500-at-christie-s.html (State of Play)

http://news.bbc.co.uk/1/hi/entertainment/3696333.stm
    (Diamond Sutra)

http://www.abovetopsecret.com/forum/thread889768/pg1
    (Ulfberhts, Chanel Handbags, Patents and Copyright)

http://www.nationalarchives.gov.uk/ (Ulfberhts, Chanel
    Handbags, Patents and Copyright)

http://www.museumofhoaxes.com/hoax/archive/permalink/
    the_feejee_mermaid (Mermaids and Sirens)

http://www.cryptomundo.com/cryptozoo-news/japanese-
    feejee-i/ (Mermaids and Sirens)

http://en.wikipedia.org/wiki/Elgin_Marbles (Did Elgin Steal
   the Marbles?)

http://www.artmovements.co.uk/artdeco.htm (What is Art
   Deco?)

http://www.vam.ac.uk/content/articles/a/art-deco/ (What is Art
   Deco?)

http://www.dailymail.co.uk/news/article-2200914/Elviss-soiled-
   underpants-fail-sell-auction--But-Bible-fetches-59-000.html
   (The Queen's Knickers)

http://www.dailymail.co.uk/news/article-2148418/Queens-
   knickers-sell-11-000-eBay-Thats-way-celebrate-Diamond-
   Jubilee.html (The Queen's Knickers)

http://www.dailymail.co.uk/news/article-2240516/Madonnas-
   iconic-conical-bra-corset-sells-30-000-auction-film-music-
   memorabilia.html (The Queen's Knickers)

http://metro.co.uk/2011/11/17/kylie-minogues-underwear-sells-
   for-5000-at-auction-229664/ (The Queen's Knickers)

http://www.artfund.org/ (Treasure Trove – The Law)

http://www.guardian.co.uk/uk/2002/aug/15/education.arts
   (Treasure Trove – The Law)

http://finds.org.uk/ Portable Antiquities Scheme (Treasure Trove
   – The Law)

http://finds.org.uk/treasure/advice/summary (Treasure Trove –
   The Law)

http://www.cites.org/eng/resources/pub/E-Ivory-guide.pdf
   (Animal, Vegetable or Mineral?)

http://www.rspb.org.uk/ourwork/policy/wildbirdslaw/
   wildbirdcrime/egg_collection.aspx (Animal, Vegetable or
   Mineral?)

http://www.defra.org.uk (Animal, Vegetable or Mineral?)

http://www.mernick.org.uk/victplas.htm (Plastic Fantastic)

http://www.bpf.co.uk/plastipedia/plastics_history/default.aspx
   (Plastic Fantastic)

http://www.plastiquarian.com/index.php?id=13&subid=146
   (Plastic Fantastic)

http://www.cgccomics.com/grading/encapsulation.asp (Comic
Book Heroes)

http://news.bbc.co.uk/1/hi/uk/3518156.stm (Comic Book
Heroes)

http://comicbook.com/blog/2011/11/29/top-10-most-valuable-
comic-books/ (Comic Book Heroes)

http://www.victoriangothic.org/the-curious-taxidermy-of-
walter-potter/ (The Death and Burial of Cock Robin)

http://www.acaseofcuriosities.com/pages/01_2_00potter.html
(The Death and Burial of Cock Robin)

http://symboldictionary.net/?p=1333 (Decoding Art)

http://www.metmuseum.org/toah/works-of-art/19.73.209
(Decoding Art)

http://www.telegraph.co.uk/news/worldnews/1555707/Beijing-
version-of-Antiques-Roadshow.html (Smash it Up!)

http://www.telegraph.co.uk/culture/art/9736648/The-man-
who-found-a-Warhol-in-a-skip.html (Warhol in a Skip)

http://www.artscouncil.org.uk/media/uploads/documents/
publications/325.pdf (Droite de Suite)

http://www.theartnewspaper.com/articles/China-debates-droit-
de-suite/28565 (Droite de Suite)

http://www.diffen.com/difference/Brass_vs_Bronze (Metal
Guru)

http://www.munknee.com/2011/03/whats-the-difference-
between-1-gold-karat-1-diamond-carat-and-1-troy-ounce/
(The Gold Standard)

http://www.gemselect.com/gem-info/carat.php (Tavernier's
Law)

http://www.dailymail.co.uk/news/article-2344801/Cast-
Napoleon-Bonapartes-death-mask-death-St-Helena-1821-
sells-170-000.html (In the Face of Death)

http://www.murdermap.co.uk/pages/cases/case.asp?CID
=643437863&Case=The-Assassination-of-Prime-
Minister-Spencer-Perceval (Bullet Point)

http://www.dailymail.co.uk/news/article-2050084/National-Museum-Health-Medicine-Bullet-killed-Abraham-Lincoln-morbid-artefacts-display.html (Bullet Point)

http://www.wartski.com/ (Bullet Point)

http://news.bbc.co.uk/1/hi/northern_ireland/7008300.stm (Key Man)

http://en.wikipedia.org/wiki/Lionel_Corporation (Do Girls Like Playing With Trains?)

http://www.bonhams.com/auctions/18092/lot/24/ (Balls)

http://www.golfer-today.co.uk/old-and-antique-golf-balls-are-valuable/ (Balls)

http://wreckandcrash.org/ (Crash Mail)

http://www.lordashcroft.com/vccollection/ (The Value of Courage)

http://www.victoriacross.org.uk/aaauctio.htm (The Value of Courage)

http://www.raaoc.com/?q=node/63 (The Value of Courage)

http://archaeology.about.com/od/cterms/qt/royal_purple.htm (purple)

http://www.guardian.co.uk/film/gallery/2012/mar/14/10-most-expensive-film-posters-in-pictures#/?picture=387273759&index=9 (Top Ten Film Posters)

http://blogs.artinfo.com/artintheair/2011/11/23/star-wars-stormtrooper-costume-sold-for-20-times-its-estimate-at-christies/ (Star Bores)

http://www.ashmolean.org/collections/highlights/?type=highlights&id=36&department=1 (Where is it?)

http://www.dhm.de/ENGLISH/sammlungen/militaria/eh181.html (Where is it?)

http://news.bbc.co.uk/1/hi/england/london/5051082.stm (Where is it?)

http://www.english-heritage.org.uk/daysout/properties/walmer-castle-and-gardens/ (Where is it?)

http://www.artloss.com/enw.guardian.co.uk/uk/2003/jul/06/arts.artsnews (Stolen to Order)

http://www.artloss.com/en (Stolen to Order)

http://www.thehindu.com/news/national/the-murky-trail-of-stolen-antiquities/article3640347.ece (Stolen to Order)

http://www.errproject.org (Stolen to Order)

http://www.independent.co.uk/news/world/americas/new-online-database-lists-nazi-loot-for-repatriation-2109768.html (Stolen to Order)

http://www.dailymail.co.uk/news/article-1031117/The-Royals-youve-NEVER-seen-The-private-photo-album-Queen-Mothers-loyal-servant-Backstairs-Billy.html (Backstairs Billy)

http://www.guardian.co.uk/money/2005/jul/02/alternativeinvestment.jobsandmoney (Tom's Time Bombs)

http://www.livescience.com/19542-forge-art-mark-landis.html (Charity Case)

http://www.themissinglist.co.uk/police-appeal/news/the-art-of-crime-fakes-forgeries-and-the-law-victoria-and-albert-museum/ (A Family Business)

http://archaeology.about.com/od/cterms/qt/Cinnabar.htm (Poison Chalice)

http://www.readingmuseum.org.uk/collections/social-history/huntley-palmers-collection/ (Empire Crunch)

http://www.bbc.co.uk/news/uk-england-berkshire-14951865 (Empire Crunch)

http://www.conwaypublishing.com/?p=5479 (Empire Crunch)

http://www.homesandantiques.com/feature/huntley-palmers-biscuit-tins (Empire Crunch)

http://england.prm.ox.ac.uk/englishness-imaging-biddenden-maids.html (The Biddenden Maids)

http://www.bonhams.com/auctions/20833/lot/278/ (Step into History)

http://www.ibtimes.co.in/articles/461227/20130425/ancient-buddhist-temple-step-record-price-sri.htm (Step into History)

http://www.antiquestradegazette.com/news/2013/feb/19/louis-vuitton-trunk-sells-for-30000/ (Luggage Label) http://www.winelabels.org/remove.htm (Etiquettes de Vins)

http://home.datacomm.ch/wineman/#Introduction (Etiquettes de Vins)

http://www.independent.co.uk/news/uk/this-britain/price-of-a-working-spitfire-heads-for-the-sky-710941.html (Spitfire)

http://www.vectis.co.uk/Page/ViewLot.aspx?LotId=457914&Section=6304&Start=60 (The Gang of Five)

http://www.collectorsweekly.com/articles/attack-of-the-vintage-toy-robots-justin-pinchot-on-japans-coolest-postwar-export/ (The Gang of Five)

http://astoundingartifacts.blogspot.co.uk/2009/06/atomic-robot-man-unknown-1949.html (The Gang of Five)

http://www.danefield.com/data/displayimage-2-352.html (The Gang of Five)

http://www.collectors-club-of-great-britain.co.uk/News/Masudaya-Gang-of-Five-Robots-Pack-a-Punch-at-Morphys/_nw540 (The Gang of Five)

http://www.nytimes.com/2006/09/12/business/media/12adco.html?pagewanted=all&_r=0 (A Complete Monopoly)

http://games.yahoo.com/blogs/unplugged/10-priciest-collectible-cards-232119394.html (Pokémon)

http://www.antiquestradegazette.com/essential-info/hallmarks/ (The History of Hallmarks)

http://www.antiquestradegazette.com/essential-info/export-licences/ (Heritage Lottery)

http://www.culturalpropertyadvice.gov.uk/ (Heritage Lottery)

http://www.artfund.org/ (Heritage Lottery)

http://www.postalheritage.org.uk/page/pennyblack (Ten a Penny)

http://www.arpinphilately.com/blog/the-penny-black-how-to-determine-its-value/ (Ten a Penny)

http://edition.cnn.com/2011/11/04/living/discovering-leonardo-salvator-mundi (Lost Leonardo)

http://www.royalmintmuseum.org.uk/collection/collection-highlights/coins/1933-penny/ (1933 Penny)

http://www.bonhams.com/auctions/19548/ (Japanese Dress Sense)
http://www.bonhams.com/auctions/17690/55457/#MR1_page_
    lots=3&r1=10&m1=1 (Japanese Dress Sense)
http://most-expensive.net/katana (Sword Play)
http://www.angelfire.com/dragon/swords/anatomy.html (Sword
    Play)
http://www.paleodirect.com/fakechinesefossils1.htm (Fake
    Dinosaurs)
http://www.independent.co.uk/news/science/bones-under-the-
    hammer-fossil-fetish-spurs-collectors-market-839427.html
    (Fake Dinosaurs)
http://www.britannica.com/EBchecked/topic/449512/
    Pembroke-table (Name Check)
http://www.woodworkforums.com/f11/18th-century-style-
    european-ash-cricket-table-97557/ (Name Check)
http://www.paulfrasercollectibles.com/News/MEDALS-%26-
    MILITARIA/2012-News-Archive/Top-5-most-expensive-
    antique-weapons/10492.page (Made to Kill)
http://news.bbc.co.uk/1/hi/world/europe/6737909.stm (Made
    to Kill)
http://www.telegraph.co.uk/news/worldnews/northamerica/
    usa/8195769/Custers-Last-Flag-sold-for-1.4-million.html
    (Flag Day)

Books

Balfour, Ian, *Famous Diamonds*, William Collins & Son,
    London, 1987
Blom, Philipp, *To Have and to Hold*, MJF Books, USA, 2004
Bondeson, Jan, *Freaks – The Pig-Faced Lady of Manchester Square
    and Other Medical Marvels*, Tempus Publishing Ltd, Stroud,
    2006
Cieslik, Jürgen & Marianne, *German Doll Encyclopedia 1800–
    1939*, Hobby House Press Inc., Maryland, USA, 1985
Crestin-Billet, Frédérique, *La Folie des Etiquettes de Vins*,
    Editions Flammarion, Paris, 2001

Fiell, Charlotte & Peter, *1000 Chairs*, Taschen, Germany, 2000

Fiell, Charlotte & Peter, *Design of the 20th Century*, Taschen, Germany, 1999

Gascoigne, Bamber, *How to Identify Prints*, Thames & Hudson, London, 1986

Godden, Geoffrey, *Godden's Guide to European Porcelain*, Random House, London, 1993

Godden, Geoffrey A., *Encyclopedia of British Pottery & Porcelain Marks*, Barrie & Jenkins Ltd, London, 1977

Grimassi, Raven, *Encyclopaedia of Wicca & Witchcraft*, Llewellyn Publications, USA, 2003

Hall, James, *Illustrated Dictionary of Symbols in Eastern and Western Art*, John Murray, London, 1994

Haussermann, Martin, *1001 Wristwatches*, Paragon Books Ltd, Bath, 2007

Hawes, Robert, *Bakelite Radios*, Chartwell Books, New Jersey, 1996

Hill, Jonathan, *Radio, Radio*, Sunrise Press, Bampton, 1993

Kitahara, Teruhisa & Shimizun, Yukio, *Robots and Spaceships*, Taschen, Cologne, 2002

Koudounaris, Paul, *The Empire of Death – A Cultural History of Ossuaries and Charnel Houses*, Thames & Hudson, London, 2011

Lambert, Sylvia, *The Ring – Design: Past and Present*, Quantum Publishing Ltd, London, 2002

Lucie-Smith, Edward, *The Thames & Hudson Dictionary of Art Terms*, Thames & Hudson, London, 1984

Mayhew, Henry, *London Labour and the London Poor*, Wordsworth Editions Ltd, 2008 (reprint of the original, 1851, 1861–62)

Miller, Judith, *The Antiques Roadshow A–Z of Antiques & Collectables*, Dorling Kindersley, 2007

Mould, Philip, *Sleuth – The Amazing Quest for Lost Art Treasures*, HarperCollins, London, 2009

Salisbury, Laney & Sujo, Aly, *Provenance: How a Con Man and a Forger Rewrote the History of Modern Art*, Penguin Books, 2010

Sibley, J.T., *The Divine Thunderbolt*, Xlibris Corporation, USA, 2009

Turner, Alexis, *Taxidermy*, Thames & Hudson, London, 2013

Ward, Pete, *The Authoritative Guide to Plastic Collectibles*, Silverdale Books, Leicester, 2001

Way, Twigs, *Garden Gnomes, A History*, Shire Publications, 2009

Whorton, James C., *How Victorian Britain was Poisoned at Home, Work & Play*, Oxford University Press, Oxford, 2011

Whorton, James C., *The Arsenic Century*, Oxford University Press, Oxford, 2010

Permissions

The *Antiques Roadshow* – A National Treasure   Statistics courtesy of the BBC *Antiques Roadshow* press department.

Bullet Point   Information courtesy of Wartski and Geoffrey Munn. www.wartski.com

Fake or Fortune Found?   With kind permission of Philip Mould OBE, www.philipmould.com

The History of Hallmarks   Specific material with kind permission of the *Antiques Trade Gazette*, www.antiquestradegazette.com

Heritage Lottery   Specific material with kind permission of the *Antiques Trade Gazette*, www.antiquestradegazette.com

Picture acknowledgements

Thanks to the following people and organisations for assisting with images:

Nicholas Halliday for the line drawings of Greek vase shapes (pages 130–3) and iconic chairs (page 161).

Biddenden Local History Society for their assistance in locating a suitable image of the Biddenden Maids (page 152).

The Donald McGill Museum for the McGill postcard image (page 178).

The Department for Business, Innovation & Skills for
permission to reproduce the Utility mark (page 190).

Useful trade and industry links

Antiques are Green, www.antiquesaregreen.org

Antiques News, www.antiquesnews.co.uk

Confédération Internationale des Négociants en Oeuvres d'Art,
www.cinoa.org

International Interior Design Association, www.iida.org

The Antique Collectors Club (Antique Collecting Magazine),
www.antique-collecting.co.uk

The Antiques Trade Gazette (ATG),
www.antiquestradegazette.com

The British Antique Dealers Association (BADA),
www.bada.org

The Association of Art & Antiques Dealers (LAPADA),
www.lapada.org

The British Antique Furniture Restorer's Association,
www.bafra.org.uk

The Antique Dealers Association of America,
www.adadealers.com

The Society of Fine Art Auctioneers & Valuers,
www.sofaa.info

The National Association of Decorative & Fine Arts Societies,
www.nadfas.org.uk

The British Hallmarking Council,
www.bis.gov.uk/britishhallmarkingcouncil

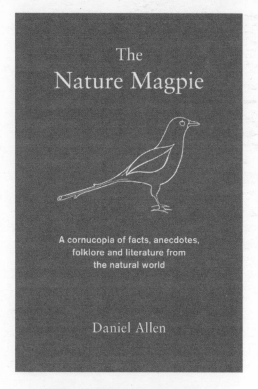

The
Nature Magpie

A cornucopia of facts, anecdotes,
folklore and literature from
the natural world

Daniel Allen

The Nature Magpie

A collection of anecdotes, facts, figures, folklore and
literature, *The Nature Magpie* is a veritable treasure trove
of humanity's thoughts and feelings about nature.

With acclaimed nature writer Daniel Allen as your guide,
join naturalists, novelists and poets as they explore the most
isolated parts of the planet, choose your side – pineapple
or durian – in the great 'king of fruits' debate and discover
which plants can be used to predict the weather.

Meet the roadkill connoisseurs, learn to dance the
Hippopotamus Polka, find out the likelihood of sharing
your name with a hurricane – and much more.

ISBN: 9781848315334 (hardback)/9781848315341 (ebook)